WRITERS
OF THE
ROUND TABLE

Editors: Norman Phillips
Sharon Fish
Richard E. Haskell
Barbara LaMarca
Don Nolte

ISBN: 978-1533240873

Published by Writers of the Round Table.
Printed by CreateSpace, An Amazon.com Company

Table of Contents

Ode to Writing
Barbie LaMarca

The air is charged with anticipation,
As nine intelligent heads bend to paper.
Hesitation, then ponderous stares,
As neurons begin to fire and summon
Bytes of data stored deep in the brain.

Then, the pens of most, the pencil of one
Start to glide across the paper.
In the background, the soft clicks and thuds
Of fingers on an iPad, typing.

If the parts communicating inside these heads
Had a sound, it would be a soft whirr,
Occasionally interrupted by a hiccup
As dissonant notions collide.

Like an intricate beehive with millions of cells
From which kernels are plucked, considered,
Thrown into the soup, or rejected and
Cast back into an empty cell.

The brew, rich with metaphors and similes
Thickened by the bias of experiences
Bland, if a paucity of emotion
Or, colorful, if a bounty of emotion,
Coalesces, and is served by its author — a unique written opus.

May 19, 2015

Who We Are, and Why We Write

We are a diverse and friendly group, and we like to write. Tuesday mornings at ten we gather at Norm Phillips' home, sit at his large, round, whimsically-carved dining table, have a little coffee or tea and light breakfast pastries, select a random prompt from folded scraps of paper, cogitate briefly and then write for twenty minutes. We take turns reading our writing to the group. Without any input from the author, the rest of us discuss the writing, not the writer. We talk about the strengths of the piece, characterization, word choice, description, honesty, humor, irony, and the list goes on. We avoid offering negative feedback. We delight in carving out two hours a week for the shared joy of creative written expression.

Norman Phillips was born in Ware Massachusetts in 1921 and lived with his illiterate Polish grandparents until he was twelve. A bright young man, he nevertheless failed his junior year of high school.

In 1942 he enlisted in the US Army air cadet program and went on to fly the P-47 in combat in Europe. He was a Colonel in the U.S. Air Force when he was shot down over Laos in 1968 while flying an F-105. After a hair-raising rescue, he retired from the Air Force, attended the University of Massachusetts, earned a BFA and an MFA, and then taught sculpture at UMass for nineteen years.

Ten years ago he was inspired to write after he attended a memoir writing program at the Exeter library offered by Nancy Eichhorn, PhD. He has published two books, the most recent, *Throw A Nickel On The Grass*, is available through Amazon or Trafford Publishing.

Following Ms. Eichhorn's methods, he hosts the *Writers of the Round Table* and continues to enjoy the writing process.

Ted King, a 70-year-old orthopaedic and hand surgeon, practiced with Access Sports Medicine and Orthopaedics in Exeter, NH, for twenty-five years. Twelve years ago he survived a right-hemisphere stroke at home while in bed. He was treated with intravenous TPA (clot buster) at Exeter Hospital within the critical three hours of onset. His therapy venues included intensive care at Lahey Clinic, inpatient rehab at Health South, and outpatient care at Portsmouth Neuro Day Rehab.

Physically active, Ted walks in his neighborhood daily and rides an adaptive recumbent tricycle in good weather. He skis at Loon and Gunstock in their adaptive programs. Ted's pre-stroke passion for competitive sailboat racing is undiminished. He participates annually in disabled sailing regattas around the country. He enjoys playing tennis with patient partners and opponents.

Ever interested in human anatomy, particularly the hand, Ted draws, paints, and sculpts hands realistically and abstractly.

An active member of the Krempels Center in Portsmouth, Ted is married and the father of two adult sons. He is a visiting lecturer at UNH's School of Health Sciences in the Occupational Therapy Department.

For **Frances L. Kane,** 1929 was memorable for two reasons: the stock market crashed and she was born. The second oldest of four was raised in Brockton, attended college in Boston, taught school for five years, and then joined Bell Telephone Labs as a computer programmer (in the days of punched cards and vacuum tubes) working four years on the SAGE System of Air Defense. She represented her company at IBM in

Kingston, NY where the ANFSQ-7 was manufactured and tested programs at bases around the country as SAGE became operational. She spent the next fifteen years as an Air Force wife, experiencing life in Wisconsin, where her son John Jr. was born, and in New Jersey while her husband John was in Vietnam, Oklahoma, New Mexico, the Philippines, and Hawaii. Following John's retirement, and a year in Duxbury, home has been Exeter, NH for 40+ years.

John J. Kane was born in Chicago in 1924. The family moved to California in 1930. John enlisted in the U.S. Army Air Corps and was commissioned a Second Lieutenant and earned his pilot's wings in February 1944. After fighter pilot training, he was assigned to the 82nd Fighter Group in Foggia, Italy where he flew fifty-one combat missions over Europe. He flew many missions escorting bombers and attacking ground targets and was awarded the Distinguished Flying Cross, several Air Medals, a Bronze Star and other awards. Before retiring  in 1973 as a Lieutenant Colonel in the U.S. Air Force, John spent time in Korea, Newfoundland, the Philippines, and Vietnam.

After retiring from the U.S. Air Force, he moved to New Hampshire in 1975 and later served for ten years as an elected Representative to the New Hampshire General Court.

Recently, he became interested in writing and is enthusiastic about the process.

Barbara LaMarca Howard is a dyed-in-the-wool Yankee who was born in Portsmouth, NH, graduated from Winnacunnet High School, earned her Psychology/Biology degree from UNH, and took additional education courses.

She was the wife of an Air Force officer for twenty years. She was a substitute teacher while her three children were in elementary school. She taught math and algebra in a private school, then math and behavior  modification to emotionally disturbed teens. She was recruited to sell furniture and did so for twenty-four years. After "retirement," she provided in-home care for hospice patients and patients with disabilities. As an aspiring entrepreneur, she recently launched "Downsize Me Gently," which strives to help people downsize and/or declutter by reorganizing and dispersing years' worth of accumulated "stuff" and "treasures."

Her three children married and created eight beautiful, delightful, little people with whom she enjoys many hours of play and enlightenment.

She is a very active member of the YMCA, loves the ocean, animals, dancing, games and spontaneity. She has boundless curiosity about and cares for the world around us.

Throughout her life, she has written journal entries, poetry and stories. Since joining the Writers of the Round Table, she has accumulated 150+ pieces of work generated by prompts. She is currently working on a children's book, called *Henry's World* and a collection of fables. She writes under her maiden name, Barbie LaMarca.

Richard E. Haskell grew up in New Hampshire, earned his Ph.D. in electrical engineering from Rensselaer Polytechnic Institute in 1963, and then spent three years in the Air Force, conducting research at the Air Force Cambridge Research Laboratories at Hanscom Field in Bedford, MA. He then joined the faculty at Oakland University in Rochester, MI where he helped establish the new School of Engineering, staying there for forty-six years, teaching a wide variety of  undergraduate and graduate courses, including courses in electromagnetic theory, coherent optics, pattern recognition, computer programming, microprocessors, embedded systems and digital design.

Along the way, he worked for General Electric in Schenectady, NY, KMS Industries in Ann Arbor, MI, served as Director of Research and Development at Industrial Holographics, Inc., Auburn Hills, MI, and spent a year at the Johnson Spacecraft Center in Houston, TX.

He is the author of over thirty books, ranging from Plasma Dynamics to Digital Design. Following his retirement in 2012, he returned to New Hampshire, joined Norm's writing group, and started writing novels.

David Johnson grew up on a cattle ranch in Wyoming, attending a two-room country school where his love for writing was instilled at an early age. A graduate of the University of Wyoming, he spent his career in finance, retiring in 2005 from John Hancock Financial Services in Boston as a Managing Director in the Bond and Corporate Finance Department.

In addition to teaching a Financial Management course for the MBA program at Southern New Hampshire University, he and his wife, Jo Lynne, are active in volunteer activities throughout the New Hampshire seacoast. When not in New England, they are often in Wyoming, enjoying the wide open spaces.

Marilyn Page is a communications coach and speaker. She's also a puppy raiser for the Guide Dog Foundation for the Blind, Inc. and speaks to various groups about the laws and etiquette for service dogs. She spent her childhood in Greenland, NH, and has lived in Massachusetts, Pennsylvania, California, Maine and Germany. She returned to Greenland in 2011 with her husband, and that set the stage for her to find the *Round Table*.

As Marilyn was working out at the gym in 2013, someone stopped to wish the gentleman on the treadmill next to her a happy birthday. Then she did the same; that's how she met Norm Phillips. As they walked, they struck up a conversation that wound its way to the topic of writing. Norm asked her if she liked to write, and when Marilyn told him that she enjoys writing speeches, Norm invited her to visit his writing group. He explained the method of writing to a prompt and Marilyn thought the process sounded interesting and challenging. At the first meeting she discovered that not only did she like the writing aspect, but also appreciated the feedback the group gave to one another. The entire process of writing to a prompt with positive critiques from a wonderful group of fellow writers has kept her coming back.

Sharon Fish grew up in Bar Harbor, ME, a place that fostered her love for the natural beauty of the ocean and its surroundings as well as the quirkiness of small-town living. As a result of her husband's career, she has lived in several states including Michigan, Delaware, Connecticut, Illinois, New York, and finally New Hampshire. At age forty she began taking college courses in Rochester, NY and completed her UNH English degree ten years later, after which she earned an education

degree from Franklin Pierce University. At age fifty-five she began teaching English at Milford High School until her retirement ten years later, in 2013. She counts those years as "her best ten years," loving her students, literature, writing, and even grammar.

She has been a member of the *Writers of the Round Table* since December 2014 and lives in Stratham, NH with her husband Blake.

Don Nolte grew up in Pennsylvania, studied German Literature at Princeton University, and then studied law at Dickinson School of Law, where he was editor-in-chief of the law review and recipient of top honors.

Don then served with the Air Force for forty-two years (twenty-six active duty then civil service) with assignments in Germany, California, New Hampshire, Texas and Alabama. He taught evening college courses in law and U.S. history.

After rowing competitively in Texas and Germany, Don founded a rowing club and coached crew in Alabama. He organized and played tuba with brass quintets in Alabama and New Hampshire.

Don's final AF assignment was as a research attorney, operating a computerized legal research system at Maxwell Air Force Base in Montgomery, AL. He became actively involved in local politics and wrote *Heartlessness of Dixie* (2016), a book pertaining to Alabama social and political issues.

Ursula Nolte grew up in Frankfurt/Main, Germany, where, as a child, she experienced the ravages of war. After two years of seminary training for church service, she went to work for a Lutheran church as a parish worker, assistant organist and youth group leader, giving music instruction to children.

She met Don when he worked for Lufthansa Airlines in Frankfurt between college years, and they married in 1968, just before he entered active duty. With the Air Force they moved seventeen times, including three tours in Germany.

Though English is not her mother tongue, Ursula took college instruction in English composition, and enjoys writing essays, often relating to her experiences in Germany.

The first section of this book is made up of three prompts written by each of us. These three prompts were selected to show our reader how an identical prompt brings out completely different stories from different writers.

Following that section are prompts that writers have chosen as their favorites.

In the final section, we have included short essays, stories and thoughts written independently, edited and not constrained by the twenty-minute time limit for the prompts. We all hope this effort will be entertaining and inspirational to the reader.

Section 1

Three Examples Showing the Diversity of Responses to the Same Prompt

Prompt: In the Hole

Oct. 20, 2015

Prompt: After Eight

June 2, 2015

Prompt: Chicken Soup

April 5, 2016

Prompt: **In the Hole**   Oct. 20, 2015
Norman Phillips

When Mario opened the door, the bell jingled. Joe looked up from his workbench, put down the hammer, spit the tacks that he held between his lips into his hand, put them down and wiped his hand on his trousers and stood.

"Hi Mario, what's up? Need your shoes fixed?"

Mario took the cigarillo out of his mouth, fixed his eyes on Joe and said, "Payday Joe." Joe's face took on an imploring look. His eyebrows lifted and his lips pouted like a parent talking to a little child.

"Mario, I – I – can't come up with the dough right now, business has been slow. You know I'm good for it. I've got a sure thing at Belmont tomorrow; it's a six to one. It'll give me enough to settle up."

"Joe, Joe, I've heard all that before. You go in and out, up and down, when you gonna learn? Sal doesn't carry deadbeats. You're in the hole for eight grand and he's getting ready to start breaking knee caps."

"Mario, haven't I been good for it before? You've been coming here for a couple of years, haven't you? And haven't I always been square with you?"

Mario relit his cigarillo, nodded and said, "Yeah Joe, you've been straight but lately that hole's been getting deeper and deeper, and Sal's thinkin' you might bail on him."

"No – no Mario! I'd never do that. I got this business going; it's just been slim pickin's lately."

"Look Joe, I ain't your friend, but let me give you a little advice. Stay the hell away from those horses; you're losing your ass."

"As soon as I get out of this hole, I'm in Mario, honest – I'm going to quit!"

Mario's face had a look of disbelief. "Okay Joe, I'll be here Saturday afternoon and you better cough it up."

Prompt: **In the Hole.** Oct. 20, 2015
Barbie LaMarca

Sam had been drifting for weeks. His whole world had come crashing down on him in a matter of hours.

The day had started with Cindy, his bride of seven months, bringing him a cup of coffee and crispy strips of bacon before his eyes could adjust to the autumn sun suffusing the bedroom with an ever-widening ray.

"What's wrong? You never bring me breakfast," he asked in a groggy voice.

"Oh, Sam! You are such a pessimist sometimes. It didn't even occur to you that it was to celebrate something exciting. We're going to have a baby!" She waved the pregnancy test strip in the air and flashed her beautiful smile.

He didn't quite know how to respond. He loved their life just the way it was. He wasn't ready to be a father. In fact, they had never even discussed having a family. "Haven't you been using birth control?" he snapped.

His hard, cold expression burst her bubble of joy; she ran out of the room, crying. "Maybe you don't deserve to be married."

Sam was too angry to talk to her, so he got dressed and left for his job at Maine Power. When he got to his cubby, there was a note on his desk from his supervisor, "Come to my office as soon as you get in."

"Have a seat, Sam. There's no good way to say this, but we have to let you go. We have to lay off 200 employees this month. I'm sorry. You'll receive five weeks of severance — one for each year of employment here. Please get your things and leave."

Sam felt like he had been punched in the gut. He gathered his things and went to his pickup in a trance. He started driving and just kept going.

Now, he was peering into a gaping, noisy space called "Thunder Hole".

In the hole is where he wanted to be.

Prompt: **In the Hole.**   Oct. 20, 2015

Frances L. Kane

We were on the big island of Hawaii, named Hawaii, and arrived at KMC, a military recreation camp, at dusk. A park ranger was scheduled to present a lecture on the Kilauea Volcano — as yet unseen to us. For me, the highlight of his presentation was to learn the ground on which we were seated was 9 feet higher than normal. Sleep that night was restless. Surely the volcano wouldn't erupt while we were there.

In the morning, I walked across the street and up a slight incline only to discover our cabin was on the edge of a steaming, hissing volcano. Looking down over 500 feet in the hole took my breath away. The diameter was over several miles across. I thought I was peering into hell.

Later that day, we drove miles around the volcano, descending past the black sands beach down to the water's edge. What had not been apparent from the top was a lava flow from the side of the volcano, moving into the sea.

One could walk up to the edge of the intensely hot lava, drive a stick into the flow, and have it ignite immediately. Most impressive, however, was the sight of lava, under the water, in flames

Truly, it was one of "the wonders of the world" and we were privileged to have been witnesses.

Prompt: **In the Hole.**   Oct. 20, 2015
John Kane

Wilford was a woodchuck. He was born in a beautiful wooded area and lived in a hole near a large tree trunk throughout his youthful life. As he grew older he began to wonder what lay beyond the boundary of his beloved woods. At the edge of the forest he could see a large farm with a barn that housed farm animals, great stores of hay and pieces of farm equipment.

While growing up, Wilford had always been interested in the world around him, and his curiosity led him to examine the barn and, perhaps, make friends with the animals who lived there. He spoke only woodchuck and would not be able to understand barks, brays and moos, but he felt that he could converse with them in some manner.

One day he discovered an opening under the barn, which led to a nice dark area that was much nicer than his hole in the woods. An added bonus was the fact that the nearby lawn provided all sorts of root, grubs and other food stuffs. He knew that he would be very happy in his new home.

Unfortunately, the farmer's wife became displeased with little mounds of dirt and holes in her lawn that were the results of Wilford's foraging. The farmer brought out his Have a Heart trap and baited it with vegetables and tasty morsels from the kitchen. That evening, Wilford foolishly fell for the ploy by entering the trap to munch on the goodies left there. The result was a loud snapping noise, and both entrances to the trap slammed shut.

The farmer came out on the following morning and found Wilford sulking in the trap. He placed the trap on his tractor and transported it way back in the forest. As it turned out, he released the woodchuck very near the site where he had grown up. As the farmer drove off toward the farm Wilford heaved a forlorn sigh.

He was back in the hole again.

Prompt: **In the Hole.**   Oct. 20, 2015
Sharon Fish

I had never felt a fluttering of sympathy for Maurice Carter, but when I heard he was about to lose his house and was in the process of filing for bankruptcy, I felt inclined to take him a home-cooked meal that he could eat in his mansion before being evicted. It was hard to imagine him in the hole as my mind ran to images of him tending his lush fruit trees, pruning, fertilizing with organic products, and picking off Japanese beetles one by one and dropping them into a plastic bag.

He had always lived alone and existed in a solitary manner, but once a year he invited a few select neighbors to join him for wassail and hors d'oeuvres the Sunday before Christmas. The piney smell of his perfect tree, ordered from L.L. Bean, mingled with the scent of lemon oil that protected his ornate mahogany furniture. Every decorative piece in the house had been chosen and displayed with precision. He loved the place, but it was all he loved.

He yelled at children who walked by, warning them away from his velvet lawn with threats of a nearby firearm. He tried to sue his neighbors, the Patricks, for erecting a plastic fence around their property. The lawsuit came to nothing, so every so often Maurice Carter would go out at night and knock over some of the interlocking sections. Naturally, the Patricks were not invited to his annual soiree. He never bought Girl Scout cookies nor gave to charities – didn't believe in them.

Now he had lost all his money in some financial scheme that had promised security. So much for the best laid plans.

I began cutting up vegetables for chicken stew.

Prompt: **In the Hole**   Oct. 20, 2015
Ted King

The sport of golf ranks up there with downhill skiing, sailing, tennis, hiking, and fishing as examples of what some might call life sports, by which, I mean sports that one can participate in throughout the span of one's lifetime.

Prior to my 2003 stroke, my wife Margie and I would frequently pass a most pleasant couple of hours playing nine holes of golf at the nearby Exeter, NH, rock farm turned golf club. I recall my game at that time featured a serious "slice," which would send my drive curving off course, to land well to the right of my intended target — it seemed perhaps a half-mile or so, from the general direction of the pin. Perhaps that is one reason why I've heard of the game of golf referred to as "a good walk spoiled!"

Since the 2003 stroke, Margie and I have not played again together. Even sadder, and symbolic of how brain injury isolates many survivors, is that my friends and neighbors have only had me out to play golf with them once! Could the reason be my remarkable slice? No, I no longer hit the ball far enough for that slice to have any serious effect.

I herewith pledge to get back at it on the driving range. Perhaps I'll someday be able to achieve that elusive, first, "hole in one!"

Prompt: **In the Hole.**   Oct. 20, 2015
Richard E. Haskell

I can't believe that I am here. The trial didn't go my way. I know that the prosecution's prize witness was lying, but now there is nothing I can do about it.

I probably should not have referred to the warden's wife the way I did this morning. That is what landed me in the hole. The warden had said, "Five days in the hole; that should keep your mouth shut."

Those were the longest five days of my life. When they finally pulled me out, I learned that the warden had died of a heart attack on my second day in the hole. Today they are burying him in a grave just outside the prison wall. From the courtyard, I watch, as they drop the warden in the hole.

Prompt: **In the Hole.**
David Johnson

In the hole, a simple phrase-
Connoting joy or else malaise.
For who you are and what you do,
You'll jump for joy or wallow blue.

In the hole - a term most dour
Of money left, a deal gone sour,
Of sleepless nights, of banker gruff,
Of struggles vain to 'mass enough.

In the hole in golfer-ese
A term of joy, a term to please,
A game of par, a game of fun,
A lucky shot, a hole in one.

In the hole in gopher-ese
A home that's snug below the breeze-
Away from cold, away from fear,
Away from threats that linger near.

In the hole a button's place,
To stay one's garb in style and grace,
A classy dress, a garment bold,
The button's there to keep and hold.

In the hole one holds an ace,
For future need to stay apace.
Lest in the hole one's score should slip,
An ace to cure in just a blip.

In the hole means many things
In time and place, in how it rings,
From bad to good, from poor to par,
Its meaning's tied to who you are!

Prompt: **After Eight**   June 2, 2015
David Johnson

Decade <u>one</u> goes all too quick,
With growth and joy and camera click,
From cradle wee to little school,
From mother's lap to swimming pool.

Decade <u>two</u> has change amore
As growth goes on, surprise in store,
From little school to college gate,
Life moves on at speeding rate.

Decade <u>three</u> and school is done.
A job is had and life is fun.
The world is there, to have and hold,
For person young, for person bold.

Decade <u>four</u> oft' brings a spouse
And kids and dog, suburban house.
As life proceeds, its pace is fast,
These days are good, but will they last?

Decade <u>five</u>, the mold is set,
For future years to life beget.
To slow up now would folly be,
Move on, move up to climb life's tree.

Decade <u>six</u> kids leave the fold,
Their decade three to have and hold,
To start new life, to pass the gate,
Their future now an open slate.

Decade <u>seven</u>, work is done
Retire, relax and have some fun.
Toil paid off along the way
Enjoy life's fruit each every day.

Decade <u>eight</u> with faith and luck,
Life goes on with jaunty pluck.
The family tree, limbs growing out
Look back now, be proud don't tout.

<u>After</u> <u>eight</u> regale life's bliss
And worry not 'bout what you miss
Life is good, the book 'most done
Look back ye now on setting sun.

Prompt: **After Eight**

Richard E Haskell

June 2, 2015

"I'm pregnant again," Mary says. Her husband, William, looks shocked.

"But we already have eight sons. Don't you think that is enough?"

"We can always use extra hands to run the farm."

William and Mary live in a house they built on Walker Creek in West Gloucester, Massachusetts. When he was twelve years old, William had sailed from England to New England with his mother, stepfather, and two brothers. The year was 1635. Now he is a selectman in Gloucester and owns forty acres of land.

A few months later, Mary gives birth.

"After eight, it's a girl! We'll name her Mary."

Mary grows into a young woman and at the age of twenty-two marries Edward Dodge. Little does she know that over 350 years from now her seventh great grandson will be writing about her at a round table in Stratham, New Hampshire.

Prompt: **After Eight**

Frances L Kane

June 2, 2015

My father attended the Lincoln school. I was raised in my grandfather's home, so I also attended the same school. It was in the neighborhood, and we all had lunch at home, returning for the afternoon session.

Recess was an important part of the day. One of the duties of the older students – in addition to being a street safety guide – was stair monitor. Maintaining a quiet atmosphere was important because junior high occupied the second floor and had a different schedule.

After eight years old, I considered myself "all grown up." In addition, although the youngest in my class, I was also at the top academically, and therefore qualified to be chosen "stair monitor." It was a very important position which required standing at the foot of the stairs leading to the girls' basement and cautioning my female classmates by sternly reciting "Quiet on the stairs, girls." Being stair monitor was probably good training for my duty later in high school where I became a "hall monitor."

To this day, when I become too officious, my husband will remind me, "Quiet on the stairs, girls."

Prompt: **After Eight**   June 2, 2015
John Kane

Ralph was an early riser. He usually woke up at six a.m. and checked the computer for mail, news and weather. After breakfast, a shower and shave, he was ready to go to work. His work day began at eight a.m. After eight, the pace of his life increased rapidly.

His work involved construction of tall buildings and most of his time was devoted to welding and bolting steel girders high above the ground. It was dangerous work that required a great amount of skill and care. His mind was constantly challenged by quick decisions. As his work day progressed he became drained of energy and began to look forward to the end of his duties. He looked forward to a nice dinner and a period of relaxation, watching television or reading a book.

After eight p.m. he was ready to retire to his bed for a good night sleep so that he would be well rested for the next grueling day.

It seemed that the hours of eight a.m. and eight p.m. were the dividing points in his life. The morning eight meant stress, and a need for constant attention, while the evening eight meant rest, relaxation and time to consider other aspects of his life.

Prompt: **After Eight**

Barbie LaMarca

June 2, 2015

"What comes after eight?" Mrs. Adams asked little Mary for the twelfth time. She took Mary's hands and put up each digit while mouthing the numbers. Last week, they had managed to get to eight after ten days of patience and encouragement.

Along with flashcards, displaying colorful animals and bold numbers, Mrs. Adams found that the use of fingers was an excuse for slipping in some much needed tactile communication.

Mary's mother had died giving birth to her. Her father, a coal miner, brought her to a convent because he couldn't stand to look at the creature that killed his wife. Laden with grief, he used the dark of the mine to subvert the dark in his mind.

By the age of two, the nuns realized that Mary was deaf. They reached out to Mrs. Adams, the local school marm, for advice. She was so taken by the sad brown eyes of the skinny waif that she decided to teach her on her own time.

Earning Mary's trust was most painstaking, but Mrs. Adams had a warmth in her smile and touch that worked its way into Mary's heart. Now, two years later, she was asking, "What comes after eight?" And Mary mouthed, "Nine."

Prompt: **After Eight**   June 2, 2015
Marilyn Page

It was already after eight a.m. and the pelican's pouch was empty. Normally, by this time he would have been full from a breakfast of tasty fish, but his routine was off this morning. He just couldn't get excited about the day. He came to the conclusion that he was bored with the sameness of each day so with that he found a quiet spot on the sandy beach and settled in.

"What would a blissful day look like?" he wondered. And his mind began to dream. . .

Well for starters, no more fishing for breakfast. I'll go to one of those fancy hotels lining the beach. I'll find a table on the patio and sit under the umbrella. Instead of fishing, I'll have the friendly waiter bring me a menu and I'll get whatever I want. It will be relaxing. After that, I'll go sit by the sparkling pool and sip one of those fancy drinks. I just hope people don't bring their dogs around me. That would be scary. Come to think of it, I hope those screaming kids don't bother me either. When I'm flying around sometimes I fly low and those kids jump up and try to grab me. Some of them even throw balls at me. Those kids are really scary creatures.

The more I think about this, it doesn't feel blissful at all. No, I think a blissful day is waking up each morning, knowing that my pelican's pouch needs to be filled, then the thrill of flying over the water, searching for the perfect fish and speeding headfirst into the water to catch the tasty rascal. Oh yes, that's a blissful day.

And with my tummy full, I found my peace, and it isn't even after eight.

Prompt: **After Eight**   June 2, 2015
Norman Phillips

After eight comes nine. It doesn't depend on what you say but what you write. Is it 'ate'? Or 'eight'? If it's 'ate,' who ate? Or what ate? Ate what? Who ate what?

'Eight' in the written form is not so ambiguous. Seven and one are always a total of eight. In the Fibonacci series of numbers, eight follows three and five and not for the logic of the addition of those two numbers but on the sequential logic of the formula for writing an ongoing stream of Fibonacci numbers.

Thus, that singular 'eight' always follows five and precedes thirteen.

As for the spoken word 'eight', one can define it as the past tense of eat because, when spoken, the correct pronunciation of the numerical number, which sequentially follows seven, is the past tense of ate, or eight.

I'm getting confused. Are we talking about time, numerical words, or what? Say the word 'eight' and what do you think of? It seems to me that at the moment of this writing, I think of 'ate' as the past tense of eat. What did I just eat? I ate at eight – that was breakfast. Now the word eight (or ate) brings to mind *what* I ate at eight and not the time I ate it.

Huh?

Prompt: **Chicken Soup**   Apr. 5, 2016
Richard E. Haskell

Chicken soup – what a lousy prompt! Who could ever write something interesting about chicken soup?

Ted seems to be typing already – must have had chicken soup in Darien when he was a kid, or maybe a hot bowl of chicken soup after a sailing race.

Sharon is writing up a storm – not sure how she can make chicken soup a downer, but I'm sure she'll succeed. Some young girl will probably choke on chicken soup.

Ursula has figured out something. They must have had chicken soup in Germany. I wonder what the German word for chicken soup is.

John is thinking – seems to be stuck. John, think of a woodchuck eating chicken soup. Still thinking. Now he's writing. Bet it will be good.

Don is really going at it. Wonder what he sees in chicken soup. Maybe some alien from outer space will be allergic to chicken soup.

Dave is busy writing. I doubt it will be a poem – nothing much rhymes with chicken soup. Maybe chicken soup was popular in Wyoming.

Barbara doesn't seem to be as stuck as I am. After all, she made up the prompt – probably writing about some grandmother making chicken soup.

Finally, Norm has about half a page written – probably one of his famous essays. The nature of chicken soup. How many ways can you look at chicken soup? How many varieties? What happened to the chicken that is now in the soup? Or maybe he's remembering the lousy chicken soup the Air Force used to serve up. That's it, chicken soup ready to eat! Great.

Gosh, I've still got several minutes to go and still can't think of anything nice to say about chicken soup.

Prompt: **Chicken Soup**   Apr. 5, 2016
Ted King

During the summer of 1970, I visited Europe. Having taken one semester of art history while a senior at Wesleyan University, I considered myself something of an art critic. For that reason, given the chance, I visited several of the great European art museums.

Having seen Andy Warhol's famous Pop art depictions of Campbell's Soup Cans while visiting the Museum of Modern Art in New York City, I fully intended to return from my first ever visit to Europe with a piece of contemporary art, and in so doing, to begin my own personal art collection.

At London's Tate Gallery, I believe I saw some comic-strip takeoffs of another Pop artist, Roy Lichtenstein. That is where I first encountered brightly colored abstract works of British silk screen artist, Anthony Benjamin.

I purchased one of Benjamin's prints and carried it home with me through London's Gatwick Airport, carefully rolled in a stiff cardboard tube, in time for the first classes of my third year of medical school.

Still pleased with this purchase today, some 45 years later, you'll find this handsomely framed, prized, abstract objet d'art hanging at the top of the stairs adjacent to our living room.

This year's "To Do" list includes having this treasured possession appraised. My hope is that it has appreciated outlandishly, to become even more valuable than Andy Warhol's Chicken Soup Cans!

Prompt: **Chicken Soup**   Apr. 5, 2016
Sharon Fish

"I've never read one of those *Chicken Soup* books," Eleanor says to her two colleagues. At the end of the school week, on a cloudy January afternoon, they are sitting at a corner table in Giorgio's Continental Bistro. "*Chicken Soup for the Soul*, she goes on, "*Chicken Soup for Teenagers, Chicken Soup for Internet Addicts, Chicken Soup for Chicken Pox*. Why doesn't someone come up with *Chicken Soup for Dealing with School Administrators*, or *Chicken Soup for Dealing with Unruly Students?*"

Final exams have just ended, and teachers are dragging. Lengthy tests that comply with Common Core Assessments sit lurking in the canvas bags awaiting the red pen and groans that will befall them later that evening.

"What about *Chicken Soup for a Bad Temper?*" Marcia pipes in. "I just want to scream when I see a shopping cart drifting in Shaw's parking lot because some inconsiderate lout is too lazy to wheel it to the corral. I am so obsessed with that rudeness that I want to start a campaign."

"God, you are both in moods," Collette says. "Maybe you'll feel better when the new semester begins; different students, fresh blood. You're mad at everyone."

"Yes. Yes, indeed I am," Marcia admits. "But, you are right. Probably I will feel better. Maybe there is a *Chicken Soup for Starting Over*. I'd read that one."

"Oh, no, you wouldn't," Eleanor says. "You wouldn't even read *Chicken Soup for Chicken Soup*. Neither would I. We like to complain too much. That's why we are drinking martinis and eating nachos."

Prompt: **Chicken Soup**   Apr. 5, 2016
Ursula Nolte

The man had lost his wife and decided to marry again. She was very pretty and had a nice personality. She could sew and keep the house clean and neat. He was very much in love with her, but did not like her cooking.

She had always prided herself on being a good cook, she had read a lot of cookbooks, and even had attended a cooking class. But whatever she made for him, he did not like.

"What can I cook for you that pleases you?" she asked him one day.

"Why don't you make a nice pot-roast?" he replied.

She bought the best cut of meat and prepared it, but to no avail, he did not like it. Then she started using spices she thought his former wife might have used. Wrong again!

Finally, one day she was so frustrated after all her futile efforts to please him, she went out and bought plain canned chicken soup. While the soup was cooking on the stove the telephone rang. It was a call from her best friend, who was very upset because her husband had left her.

It took her quite a while to calm her friend down. When the call ended she rushed to the kitchen because she could smell that something was burning. It was the chicken soup. The liquid had mostly evaporated.

As fast as she could, she saved the rest. "Oh," she thought, "I don't have time to prepare another meal; I'll have to serve this to him." Reluctantly, she brought the tureen to the table.

To her surprise, he ate it with delight and asked: "What spice did you use? This is exactly what my dear Anna had in her dishes."

Prompt: **Chicken Soup**   Apr. 5, 2016
John Kane

    Sally was a young single woman known for her warm personality and her ability for interesting conversation. She also had a reputation as a wonderful hostess and cook. She worked in an office, and she frequently invited her office friends to dinners that were socially pleasant and always featured delicious meals.

    One day a new employee appeared on the scene. His name was Allen. He was a young man, somewhat handsome, with a nice personality, and Sally was immediately attracted to him, and she decided to invite him to the next dinner.

    In due time, Sally sent the dinner invitations, and she decided to devote a special effort in planning for this meal. It should include an attractive salad, one or two side dishes, and her favorite specialty, chicken soup.

    When the day of the dinner arrived, Sally sprang into action. She made an extra effort to set an attractive table illuminated by the usual wax candle display. The dinnerware and silverware were accompanied by carefully folded linen napkins. The table was ready for the guests.

    The guests took their seats and Sally brought the food to the table. The last item was a large tureen of chicken soup. She mentioned the fact that it was her favorite recipe, to which most of the guests responded with complimentary remarks as she presented each steaming bowl. When she brought Allen's serving, he politely declined, much to her surprise and obvious disappointment. Allen explained, "When I was a boy I grew up on a chicken farm in Oklahoma. When I finally left home, I vowed that I would never again eat another bowl of chicken soup."

Prompt: **Chicken Soup**   Apr. 5, 2016
Don Nolte

She sat comfortably ensconced in a plush, well-worn easy chair, a book on knitting lying on the small table to her side, a sturdy lamp with a frayed antique shade casting light upon the handiwork she was engaged in.

"Good morning, Gramma," I said as I held the screen door open a few inches.

"Come on in, dear," she beckoned. Visiting my grandmother was one of my favorite things to do, a short drive to her house, with a sense of time warp, as I put the techno-complexities of modern life behind me to savor her calm, loving presence.

"I'm just doing a little knitting," she said, "I was looking forward to you coming by."

As we sat there chatting about whatever came to mind, a sense of belonging came over me. Yes, I belonged here, in the glow of her unquestioning spirit.

Then I got to what I really needed to talk about. "I hate to burden you with this" I said, "but I need to talk to someone. Yesterday they gave me my marching orders – they wished me a happy life, just not in the company. I lost my job. And now I don't know what to do."

"Well, honey, that has happened to a lot of people, your grandpa for example. He always said 'There's no such thing as a problem, just an opportunity to excel.' He used his time between jobs to figure out what he did best. He went back to school for a while, and emerged in a totally new career, in which he blossomed."

"I'd like to think I could do that, Gramma, but I'm not – I'm just not sure. I feel awfully nervous; I didn't sleep well last night."

"Are you hungry, dear? Would you like something to eat?"

"Well, I guess I am."

Next to a good night's sleep, there's one thing that cures your ills and will help you find your way – grandma's chicken soup.

Prompt: **Chicken Soup**   Apr. 5, 2016
David Johnson

Ethel was a hard worker. Wearing a feather boa, she spent endless days and nights on the assembly line alongside her co-workers, cranking out products for a demanding employer and a hungry public. The factory was located in Shell Creek, a small mid-western town where everyone worked for, or was related to, someone who worked for the plant.

A steady stream of raw materials flowed into the plant from the rail siding adjacent to the manufacturing floor. Ethel and her associates efficiently converted them into a usable and nutritious food that nearly every American ate on a daily basis. There was no workers union at Ethel's plant. She and her co-workers toiled night and day in tight quarters with a zero tolerance for less than perfect performance.

Ethel was a chicken. She spent her short life at Chicken Little, Inc.'s egg laying facility in Shell Creek, alongside 250,000 of her closest friends all of whom were bred for maximum egg production. One day, Ethel and the seven other chickens with whom she had shared a three foot square cage for over a year were summarily removed and put on a truck to Soup Creek, a neighboring town and home to Souperior Soup, a subsidiary of Chicken Little, Inc. You see, now that Ethel's productive life was over, she was a "spent hen" destined for the cannery. Say a prayer for Ethel the next time you dine on canned chicken soup.

Prompt: **Chicken Soup**   Apr. 5, 2016
Barbie LaMarca

C is for the Chicken whose life was taken.
H is for the Heat from the pot belly stove.
I   is for the Ingredients of which there are many.
C is for the Cornbread accompanying the soup.
K is for the cast iron Kettle in which it is boiled.
E is for the Escarole and other nutrient rich greens.
N is for the Nourishment the soup will provide.

S is for Simmering for two or three hours.
O is for the Onions which will cure many ills.
U is for Ultimate satisfaction when tummies are full.
P is for the Pleasant associations when we think of homemade chicken
    soup.

Prompt: **Chicken Soup**   Apr. 5, 2016
Norman Phillips

Bob Campbell's nickname was "Soup". He didn't seem to mind being called "Soup" because none of us kids had a derogatory feeling about Campbell. After all, in the late 1930s Campbell's soups were on every grocery shelf and working people ate them daily. They were good but by today's standards and tastes, way too salty. But back then, what did we know? That was the era when dietary concerns never made it into the squawking radio news nor the newspapers.

Even in high school, diet was never the subject brought up by our good but poorly paid teachers. Oh, it was life back then, the way it should be! Don't we all look back at those days?

When the May sun and the June calendar page pushed back memories of snowball fights and sledding on the steep, snow packed streets, our hijinks followed us to our favorite swimming hole. It was called that, but it wasn't really a hole. It was a frisky brook that had been dammed, letting the water fill the generous depression, lovingly sculpted into a beam-lined natural swimming pool. The bachelor who lived nearby was a railroad engineer who had created an idyllic swimming hole with the materials he scrounged from the railroad and with the help of a volunteer labor force of young guys who loved swimming.

Red Prevost had set telephone poles connected by cable from which he had hung a trapeze. On one side he built a tall structure with a platform on top where a long pole with a stiff iron rod attached was able to hook the trapeze, draw it to the platform from which we'd launch ourselves over the water.

As we grew accustomed to the gymnastics possible on that trapeze, we did somersaults and gyrating flights to splash into the cool, forgiving water.

Soup Campbell, who really wasn't a swimmer, came with us one day. Soup usually spent the summer on the tennis court. When we encouraged him to try the trapeze, he reluctantly did.

"Do a somersault Soup!" we yelled.

He was afraid, and wouldn't, so after that we called him "Chicken Soup".

Section 2

Selected Prompts:

Some of our Favorites

Prompt: **A Journey and I Want ...**   Jan. 11, 2011
Norman Phillips

I started on this journey five years ago. I started drawn by something I didn't understand, but the space that drew me embraced me and I felt wanted. Wanted because I began to remember moments, experiences, hopes and fears that I felt were worthy of sharing with others. So I started to write.

It came out like a torrent once I learned how to open the floodgates. Those mental blocks or gates usually keep some or most of life's experiences deep in the shadowy corners of our minds – often held by restraints that we put there to keep them at bay.

Those singular moments and experiences are in there, piled on high, categorized by the measurement of calendars. 1938, '39, '40, Pearl Harbor, World War II, and then there is the geography: North Africa, Italy, Corsica, France and Germany.

On and on, page after page, then to be stitched together, connected for others, to help them to understand, to believe, to feel and to enjoy.

And this brings me to the end of that journey – I want to finish. The compelling reason that caused me to accumulate these scenes was my insatiable desire to experience everything there was, and then I felt a need to get them out, to share them with others. Now that that is done, I must detach myself from them and draw them into a collage that carries balance, coherence, creativity and entertainment.

A goal to entertain seems to depreciate a lengthy effort, but ultimately, what reason would draw another person to read my words?

This part therefore, the writing that is, must be done, and it must be done in a way that does not deprecate or devalue those parts for which the story is written.

Prompt: Creativity June 16, 2012
Norman Phillips

Some people think that creativity is something that artists possess. It might be helpful to think of it as an evolutionary component of humans' highly developed brain – something that is there in the physically mature entity that has been brought to life and enters the world with other members of its species.

But for the human organism to survive in prehistoric eras, that brain had to be capable of absorbing external stimuli, and with its accretion of data, of organizing it, classifying it and making judgments that favored survivability. Thus it was that brainpower became more than the simple adding of known stimuli. Judgment results when miscellaneous experiences are synthesized so that a desirable outcome can obtain from disparate hard facts.

Since observable or physically experienced stimuli do not always yield a predictable result, the human organism begins to question, to wonder, to say to itself "what if?"

The resultant answer to "what if?" has an unlimited dimension exploitable to those that continue to keep asking questions about possibilities.

Prompt: What Does a Whisper Look Like?
Norman Phillips

"The branches are whispering," she said.

I looked at BG and said, "What do you mean, 'they're whispering'? BG's face brightened. "Can't you see that? They're whispering in that breeze. Look, the leaves are doing a slow dance up there, and they don't even know we're down here."

BG always had a quirky way of looking at things – no, I don't mean *looking*; I mean *saying* what she was looking at. She seemed to see the sides of things that other people never saw – at least not until she told them what she'd seen.

BG bent her head way back and took a deep breath. "Isn't it wonderful out here? Those leaves know they're going to be dropping off pretty soon, but they're getting themselves ready to show off before they leave their cousins."

"What do you mean their cousins? They're all the same up there."

She interrupted, "No they're not! Look, see those big branches? And then the smaller branches? Those are the uncles and aunts – and further up, those little branches are theirs and — then the little leaves are like *kids* so they're all cousins to each other."

"What's that got to do with the branches whispering?" I asked sarcastically.

"Oh Mr. Practical. Don't you ever see things the way mother nature made them?"

"Mother nature? Come on BG, get real, they're just old maple trees that turn red and orange and the leaves will fall off and the tree gets dormant till next spring."

"Yes, but then they give us the sweet maple syrup to remind us of how beautiful it all is."

Whisper didn't have more nightmares than other children and after she entered high school she began to feel that she was part of the galaxy of children that came every day in the bright yellow school buses and clattered trays and talked loudly in the cafeteria. She was still called Whisper, but she felt herself being drawn toward her classmates – particularly the boys.

Whisper couldn't keep herself from judging the popular, loudmouthed boys around whom most of the girls swirled, but there was one who got her attention. He was quiet but not the same way that Whisper was quiet. He had a calm, unflappable manner that seemed to regard the goings-on as beneath him.

He was big enough to be an athlete, but he never tried out for any of the teams.

Teachers liked him. He always had his homework done, and he aced the exams.

Prompt: A Word that Begins With ...   Apr. 15, 2014
Norman Phillips

A word that begins with any letter is a word, there's none better.

When written, that first letter opens a door, there are possibilities to explore.

First letter, a vowel, followed, but not always.

"A" is such, it can stand alone.

"I" another and then there's "U", spoken not written, or you'll misconstrue.

I switch from written to spoken. Aren't they the same?

Consonants are different, never alone, mostly followed by a vowel, like a dog after a bone.

Is there one that stands alone? Only a vowel like "I", which stands for me, we are vowels together. Unable to change from one to two, one to too – -too many choices for my ears to hear, yet when written, they all are clear.

Words are something. But what do they mean?

An endless variety, thoughts yet unseen.

Something else propels them forward, the unwritten, unspoken words, the meaning moving forward, other meanings not heard or seen, for each word, known, serene.

Prompt: Tombstone   June 24, 2014
Norman Phillips

The markers used to identify where a particular person is buried range from the grandeur of Egyptian pyramids to the improvised, simple cross now seen in Western movies. That cross is made of branches found nearby or simply a board driven into the head of the grave.

Military cemeteries mark their deceased with identical stones in the shape of a cross and the name of the deceased. Stones for members of the Jewish faith carry the Star of David instead of the Christian's cross.

Our cemeteries are filled with a variety of stones ranging from the flat plaque lying on the ground to mausoleums echoing Greek designs. Some are carved with ornate figures or images, and the words one can find on tombstones range from Homeric praise to everyday humor.

To whom is it important to have a tombstone that serves as something more than a mere identification?

"We are not the same," is what tombstones say, mine is bigger than yours. I am the King and my tomb shall rise grander than my predecessor's.

The expense and human effort to create tombstones that exceed the need to mark a particular grave reveals humanity's tendency to look back, to remember, rather than to look forward by pushing the past behind.

What's dead is dead and that's all it is.

Prompt: **Sea Glass**   Sept. 22, 2015
Frances L. Kane

Smooth as a stone, worn by the tide, sand, and weather, stored and displayed, priceless and beautiful.   That is a description of sea glass. Whose eye hasn't spotted a colorful piece while walking along the shore and felt compelled to stop, admire, and pick it up?

One wonders about its origin: how long might it have been in the ocean and why was it abandoned? Was it once a bottle with a message or once a bottle idly thrown overboard? How many years did the sea take to reduce it to its small size?

Singly – not impressive – but collectively, a thing of beauty resting on the mantle, it is a reminder of all those years walking the beaches of this earth.

Prompt: **Ode to Our Maple Tree**   May 19, 2015
Frances L. Kane

It was so large and leafy.
It was six feet across.
It was over 200 years old.
It was our air conditioner.
And now it is gone.

The decision was not ours,
But the electric company's.
Bags of leaves in the fall – but a memory.
No more squirrels on the roof.
No more gutters to clean.

But mostly missed is
The beauty and massiveness
That graced our home.
It has kept our friend warm all winter.

Prompt: **The Rain on the Roof**   Dec. 8, 2015
Frances L. Kane

Some of the best memories of my childhood are from those summers spent at Duxbury Beach. We were so carefree! The beach sits on a narrow piece of land that extends fourteen miles from Green Harbor to Gurnet Light in Plymouth.

One never knew what changes the weather might bring. Gathering driftwood was always a challenge. When a northeaster blew, we fired up "Old Bertha", the pot-bellied, cast iron stove that sat in a corner of the front room, and found a comfortable spot to read a good book while listening to the rain on the roof. There was no attic – just exposed beams, which intensified the sound.

If the storm arrived at high tide, the waves could reach the front porch. I remember praying the strong winds would not topple the cottage, which had been rebuilt from previous storms. The back of the house faced the marsh. There were times when the ocean met the rising water. Luckily, I missed those events!

Once, my sister's friend decided she would sleep on the beach – only to be driven inside during the night by a sudden storm. Her last words when she left the house with her sleeping bag had been, "I'll send you a postcard from Provincetown!"

Prompt: **Down the Cobblestone Alley**   Mar. 22, 2016
Frances L. Kane

Some stories are etched in your mind forever. My grandfather recalled the molasses flood in Boston, and passed on the memory of that fateful time to us when we were children. To this day, people swear that on a hot, humid day, one can smell the sweet odor of molasses rising out of the cobblestones.

Molasses was one of the staples at the turn of the century. It was shipped into Boston Harbor from Puerto Rico and stored in a large 50-foot by 90-foot steel tank which held two million gallons. On January 15, 1919, the poorly constructed tank ruptured, pouring its sticky contents down cobblestone alleys in a 15-foot wave moving about 35 mph toward the water. It was a dreadful event in the history of Boston. Twenty-one people died, 150 were injured and animals lost their lives in its path. Buildings were destroyed and the elevated railway buckled. It took months to clean up the gooey mess, which was spread all over the city.

The Great Molasses Flood is noted every year in the press and in the minds of those who have heard the story, passed on through generations. If you are ever in the North End on a hot humid day, stop and sniff – especially if you go down a cobblestone alley. There may be a bit of history lingering in the air.

Prompt: **A Knock at the Door**   Feb. 2, 2016
Frances L. Kane

In the fifties, Beaver Dam Lake in New York was sparsely settled by both year-round residents and summer homes. It was a heavily wooded area. My house was surrounded by woods except for the log cabin next door which was used only during July and August.

My home was on a ridge, high above the lake. The house at the corner had a fenced yard for their large dog who was kept outdoors. I, too, had a dog named "DD" – short for damned dog – inherited from the previous tenants.

One cold winter night, during a raging blizzard, there was a pounding at the front door. I was 26, alone and alarmed. However, I felt that someone out in bad weather in the middle of the night must need help.

To my surprise, when I opened the door, I was faced with the huge, shaggy dog from the corner. He must have been aware that "DD" was snug and warm inside. After he entered the room, I brought him a bowl of water, made him a bed, and lit a fire in the fireplace. He settled down and remained there for the night. "DD" slept on my bed.

In the morning, his attitude changed; he didn't want to leave. He had found the perfect port in a storm. Because I had to go to work, I finally coaxed him out the door with dog food. To this day, I'll never know how he knew he could find a warm place or if he was aware "DD" lived there. I had never seen him walk by with his owner. Perhaps his animal instincts led him to my door. He never returned.

Prompt: **An Ode to a Flea**   May 19, 2015
John Kane

Alexander was a flea. He was born into an upper crust family of fleas that lived in a large manor house in a fine neighborhood.

Alex grew rapidly into his early life and learned to perform all the functions of a youthful flea. There were many things to learn about the society of fleas. He became aware of the dangers of being swatted and of techniques to avoid the claws of cats and dogs who were scratching perilously close.

Alex grew into adult fleahood and could cope with sudden violence. He was aware of the rampant acts of discrimination against fleas and learned to avoid the deadly effects of poisonous flea powders. Life was good but there was one thing that would make it better. He yearned for the day when he would have a dog for his very own.

One happy day a new thoroughbred puppy was brought home to the house. Before any of the other fleas could lay claim to the new pup, Alex sprang to the fur on the pup's leg. After a while, he had traversed the entire pelt and he issued warnings to other fleas who might trespass on his domain. It was most satisfying to have one's own dog.

Things went well in the relationship. The pup was hardly aware of the flea's presence and Alex was free to crawl through the fur without being detected. All was going well until the fateful day that tragedy came upon the scene. The home owner decided that the pup needed a bath. In the process Alex was flushed from his domain and disappeared down the drain.

We should compose an ode to Alex, a flea of renown, who was envied for having a dog of his own.

Now he is in darkness that is smelly and dank and is wondering how to escape from this tank.

The unfairness of it all has fostered his wrath. He was an innocent victim of a puppy's first bath.

Prompt: **It Is Time**   Oct. 27, 2015
John Kane

Ann was in a state of sorrow and desolation brought on by the event of her mother's death. She could not force herself to accept the fact that she would no longer be able to enjoy the caring love and the sense of belonging that was so important to their relationship. Ann could only think of her girlhood days when her mother was her guiding light as she moved into adulthood. Her mother could be counted upon to be soft and cuddly but firm as a stone when the situation called for it. It was so important for a girl to have a role model and her mother was that – in spades.

The relationship became even more intense when she married and was raising her two children whom "Gran" adored and spoiled as only a loving grandma can do. She enjoyed reading children's books to them and could be counted on for trips to movies, parks, zoos and other events of interest to children. In time, grandma aged and slowly began to need the care and attention that she gave to her daughter in earlier years. That role reversal served only to intensify their deep feelings for each other.

As Ann sat there remembering the happy times, these thoughts were overcome by the overwhelming grief facing her. Her mind dwelt upon the fact that today's funeral would be the last time she would be able to view her mother. She was concerned about the way in which her children would be able to cope with their first true experience of deep sorrow.

The door opened and her husband entered the room. He walked over, placed his arm around her shoulder, and gently said, "Ann, it is time to go."

Prompt: **Twilight**   June 16, 2015
John Kane

Poets have claimed that the dawn comes up like thunder, but the word twilight is spoken as a more tranquil time in our lives. One description prepares us for the noise and activity of the coming day, but the other promises the tranquility found in the state of relaxation and reflection.

Many people have a problem with the act of winding down at the end of the day's activities. They have not come to realize the comfort and pleasure of relaxing with family or friends in a different setting of conversation. In the twilight hours, the human psyche is programmed to modify the inner self by placing the day's activities into the memory bank. This clears the mind for the next day's activities.

The fast pace of most American lives have produced a culture that provides little time for the twilight hours. The pleasures of twilight time are erased by the electric light, the television set and tasks involving homework to prepare for the next day.

Fortunate is the person who has organized personal affairs, so as to reserve those magic hours of twilight for actions that will serve to make tomorrow a better day.

Prompt: **Bats in the Belfry**   May 3, 2016

John Kane

Reverend Spenser was well regarded in his small town, both as a religious leader and a public personality. His Sunday sermons were noted for their relationship to day-to-day problems.

One day in a meeting with some church members, a few ladies made comments concerning the bats who occupied the spire of the church. They suggested that the bats were a possible source of disease and offered an offensive presence. The pastor gave it some thought and decided it would be a worthy subject for a Sunday sermon.

When the people arrived for Sunday service, they walked past a large cage containing a few bats. The children were fascinated, but the older people just smiled and wondered what the reverend had in mind. When it came time for the sermon, the reverend began by recounting his conversation with the ladies. He accepted their point of view, but he offered another thought for consideration. He began by stating we are all God's creatures and the bats were part of all the creatures on earth. Bats were given a food supply that included mosquitoes and other nocturnal insects that annoyed or harmed humans.

He suggested that we should believe that bats were led to occupy churches by some divine force. He drew some laughter when he noted that the bats were always present at church on Sundays. He admired them as fellow creatures of God. He ended the sermon by saying that the janitor would be asked to keep the belfry reasonably clean for the benefit of the members of the church, as well as our bat friends in the belfry.

Prompt: **Under the Old Willow Tree**   Jan. 12, 2016
David Johnson

From the Brooklyn apartment where Steven and his family lived all he could see was the brick wall of the tenement across the alley. If he craned his head at the right angle, Steven could see a large willow tree growing in a small park across the street. Years ago, someone had built a wooden bench that encircled the trunk of the tree, and it was a gathering place for neighborhood folks of all ages. Steven would while away the hours under the old willow tree, reading, playing with his friends and daydreaming about life beyond the confines of the Brooklyn neighborhood from which he rarely ventured.

A favorite book of Steven's was *Under the Old Willow Tree*. It told the story of Sven, the young son of a pioneer family settling in the wilds of Minnesota in the 19th century and the life they lived in the shadow of an old willow tree. The tree was the deciding factor in Sven's father's decision to build the family homestead where he did. It provided shade and a bit of greenery in the otherwise treeless prairie.

Sven spent hours under the tree, reading, playing with his siblings and daydreaming about life beyond the farm's confines. One of his favorite books was *My Life in the City*, a story about Steven, a young man growing up in a Brooklyn tenement where all he could see was the brick wall of the adjacent building and a glimpse of a willow tree, a bit of greenery in an urban environment. Sven fantasized about Steven and the exciting world of the city that lay at his doorstep.

Steven and Sven were two young men living in different environments, each fantasizing about life beyond the horizon of his insular world. How disparate their lives were – or were they? While Steven's urban environment differed greatly from Sven's rural surroundings, they, and their family and friends, gravitated to one thing, an old willow tree. In this case, the willow tree was a focal point, the glue that pulled and held people together. Whether it's in the midst of a city or on the empty prairie, the tree is symbolic of our need for a place of belonging, a constant in an ever changing world.

Prompt: **I Am Who I Am**   Sept. 22, 2015
David Johnson

I AM WHO I AM

I am who I am
Said the roach to the bee,
So take me as is,
'Cuz I am what you see.

I don't make things sweet,
Oft' I'm met with an "OOH!"
But take me as is,
For the job that I do.

You pollinate well,
A most worthy chore,
For flowers and food,
From mountain to shore.

But take me as is,
While I tidy what's left,
Of crumbs large and small,
In crevice and cleft.

For every nice bug
And critter you see,
Just slightly offstage,
Lurks a critter like me.

Cleaning debris,
Despite what they say,
To make the world better,
In most every way.

Prompt: **Three Pennies, Two Dimes, and a Quarter**   Apr. 14, 2015
Richard E. Haskell

"That will be fifty cents," the clerk said.

Billy reached into his pocket and pulled out three pennies, two dimes, and a quarter.

"That's only forty-eight cents." The clerk seemed annoyed.

"But that's all I've got," Billy said.

"Well then I guess you have to put the card back."

"But it's for my mother's birthday."

"Too bad, you need two more cents."

An old lady was standing behind Billy. "Here is two cents."

"Thanks," Billy said.

He paid the clerk, took the card, walked outside and sat on the bench. He took out the card and signed his name.

The lady who gave him the two cents walked out of the store and sat next to Billy on the bench.

"That's really nice of you to buy a card for your mother's birthday,"

"Are you somebody's mother?" Billy asked.

"Yes, my son was your age a long time ago."

"Did he give you birthday cards?"

"Yes, and I still have them in an old shoe box at home."

"So does my mom. I'm really glad you had two cents," Billy said.

"This is the most I have ever gotten for two cents," she said.

Prompt: **The Yellow Balloon**   Nov. 10, 2015
Richard E. Haskell

Jim and Joe are two radio waves, each of slightly different frequencies, belonging to two different cable networks, streaming their way from the communication satellite 22,000 miles above the earth, on their way to a TV station on the ground in central Texas.

"Hi Jim, I haven't seen you in some time. What are you carrying today?"

"Joe, it's some stupid sitcom. I guess it makes people laugh, but I think it is inane. What are you carrying?"

"I'm on my way to an all-news network, and I'm carrying some breaking news about a terrorist group who just blew up an airplane at 32,000 feet."

"Boy, that's not good. You wonder what the world's coming to."

"What's that off to our left? It looks like a big yellow balloon."

"It sure is pretty against the blue sky."

"You know, I love this journey from the satellite to earth. It is so relaxing and beautiful."

"I agree. It is a lot easier than getting stretched and squeezed when they are putting the information into us."

"Well it looks as if we're almost there."

When they reach the station, Joe gets squeezed and pushed again, this time onto a videodisk ready for broadcast to the nation. He gets a feeling of satisfaction as he hears the message that he has been carrying sent out over the airwaves:

"We interrupt this program to bring you breaking news."

Prompt: **His Expression Strikes Me as Kind**   Oct. 13, 2015
Richard E. Haskell

His expression strikes me as kind, his deep blue eyes welcoming me, his oversized ears appearing to make it easier for him to hear me, his broad smile reassuring me that it was not a mistake for me to come, meeting him for the first time here in Dot's Café, a café filled with the luncheon crowd, a meeting I have been dreading, not wanting to be disappointed one more time, having been disappointed ten previous times, but deciding to give *match.com* one last chance.

I held out my hand. "Hi, I'm Janice."

Prompt: **It is Time**   Oct. 27, 2015
Richard E. Haskell

"It is time to go to the rehearsal dinner." My daughter's tone was emphatic.

My granddaughter, Sophie, is getting married tomorrow. I have mixed feelings about the gathering, coming as it does only six months after my husband died, and the secret I have kept from my daughter and granddaughter still haunts me.

Sophie met Dave, her husband to be, at college two years ago, and I am very fond of him. Still, my first granddaughter getting married is a big event for me.

"Hurry up, mom. Sophie will be here any minute to pick us up."

Sophie walks into the room and my heart nearly stops. I am frozen for several seconds.

"Where did you get that necklace?" I ask.

"Dave gave it to me."

"Where did he get it?"

"His father gave it to him. He said it is a family heirloom, handed down by his grandfather. Why do you ask?"

I feel short of breath. "That's my necklace," I whisper.

"How can it be your necklace?" Sophie asks.

"It was taken from me a long time ago."

"Who took it from you?"

"A soldier."

"Where?"

"Auschwitz."

Prompt: **Ted's Painting**   Mar. 31, 2015
Sharon Fish

This is what he heard him say: "Ted's painting will stay in the locker room the entire season. I want you boys, you athletes, to know that this is a team sport, and when you go out on the field, you are together; you are extensions of one another. Nod to your mother in the stands because she brought you into this world, and point to the heavens to acknowledge that whatever talent you have is God-given. Don't show off. If by some lucky chance we win a game, the victory sign will be our team gesture. And whether we win or lose, we show the opposing team the sign of peace, and we will mean it – no hard feelings no matter the outcome and no matter what has transpired during the game." Andrew's baseball coach worked every player hard, but he always figured the coach, his uncle and father-figure, was hardest on him.

As a teenager, he had drawn that same image of two hands, one index finger pointing upward, and the first two fingers of the other hand splayed in a V, over and over again, starting at the end of February all the way through the end of May when the varsity season ended. He saved all his copies and stashed them in an old moving box in the corner of his bedroom closet, finally poring over them after his college graduation when his mother insisted that either he purge or she would. Still, he couldn't part with them, some drawn in pencil, others in markers or highlighters – the colors vibrant and resonant, the symbolism even stronger.

He assembled a collage of his renderings and had it framed by an old craftsman he had met at church. It turned out to be a large piece that loomed over his sunlit corner desk on Wall Street and reminded him daily of his coach's pregame talk about Ted's painting.

Prompt: **It Is Time**   Oct. 27, 2015
Sharon Fish

Clutching her white parka close around her while trying to zip it, she walked through the dark shopping center parking lot where she had just finished her six-hour shift at Market Basket. Inserting the key into the Jeep door (the remote lock had not worked in years) she shivered at the prospect of what was next. "It is time," she thought, "to get a few hours of rest."

She drove to the Walmart Super Store on Amherst Street where the parking lot lay nearly empty and settled on a remote spot behind the store near a street lamp, pulled into a marked space, turned off the ignition, opened the driver's side door, got out and opened the back of the Jeep. Unfolding several tired-looking blankets and a king-sized pillow, she thought about how she would arrange her bed. Ultimately, she decided to lie across the back seat facing the street lamp so that she would be alert to any danger.

She placed two of the folded blankets neatly on the brown cloth seat and wrapped herself tightly with the third. She reached over the front seat to grab a loaf of cinnamon bread and a bottled water and lay back, her head propped on her pillow, and began eating. Then she pulled her cell phone from inside her jacket pocket and set the alarm for three hours, when it would be time to move on.

Prompt: **Under the Old Willow Tree**   Jan. 12, 2016
Sharon Fish

Plump as a plum and dark as coffee, Ma Zuma sat under the old willow tree on a corner property in the Garden District of New Orleans. Adeline and Henry Lafayette, the wealthy free spirits who lived in the refined white house with its tall windows and wrought iron balconies, did not mind. In fact, they thought Ma Zuma added a certain charm and often brought her a cup of chicory coffee or a glass of sweet tea.

Ma plunked herself down under the tree at 10:00 a.m. and stayed there until 2:00, watching the tourists gawk at the pedigreed elegance of the old neighborhood that had been barely touched by the infamous Hurricane Katrina. From the pockets of her tent-like calico dress she withdrew a variety of voodoo dolls and other talismans and would begin muttering as soon as an out-of-towner came near – and she could spot them a mile away in their button-downs, leather Birkenstocks, garish T-shirts, and the newest iPhone with Selfie Stick, wanting their friends back home to envy their brush with Southern gentility.

So when Ma started her muttering and incantations, her prey avoided looking directly at her, expecting the evil eye, or worse. But she cajoled them. "I'll bet you'd like to feel passion again, or maybe dole out some well-deserved retribution, Honey." Her voice was soft but clear, and the out-of-towners would slow down, look at her wares, and want to touch the chicken claw or the tiny death-like dolls.

"What's on your mind, Honey?" she would ask when she saw their eyes fixed on her remedies. "They ain't gonna hurt ya', they gonna help ya.'

"My husband ran off with his secretary," one woman told her.

Ma held up a doll and said, "Mail this to the secretary. They'll both regret the infraction, Honey."

At 2:00 p.m., Ma Zuma counted her day's earnings, tucked her remaining merchandise back into her big pockets and headed off to Bourbon Street.

Prompt: **Gone in an Instant**
Sharon Fish

Oct. 6, 2015

It never occurred to Angie that she would spot a snake sunning itself on the hood of her red Jeep, although it had crossed her mind that she might see her neighbor's cat Sophie doing so. In any case, Angie just looked at the snake and said, "It's up to you what you do, but I am going to the shed to fetch a shovel and don't mind a few more dings in my jalopy." The snake pondered a minute and then reared its diamond-shaped head, turned around and slithered down the grill and into the tall grass – gone in an instant.

"Smart reptile," Angie called after the creature. She wondered if that encounter was going to set the tone for the day. She was, after all, on her way to her lawyer's office, a snake of a different kind, as far as she was concerned. She dreaded the crisp, modern office, cold as a reptile's blood, the secretary, now called an administrative assistant, in her designer suit, and her attorney, smug and oily, who claimed there was nothing he could do about restoring her dignity, getting her what she deserved in the ugly divorce engulfing her.

There she was, forty years old, in her best dungarees and wool sweater, at the mercy of these folks who probably thought her husband was right to high-tail it out of Dodge. He, too, was gone in an instant, almost. She wanted what people called closure, and her small ranch, her jeep, and her pride.

"Mr. Connors will see you now, Ms. Sullivan," said Jennifer, the willowy receptionist.

"I have some bad news," Connors growled.

"Try again," said Angie.

Prompt: **Key**   Apr. 29, 2014
Marilyn Page

The key to a prompt is to get the creative juices flowing, to create a story about something you might never have considered.

It reminds me of the little girl Ruthie who kept the key to her clubhouse on a braided necklace she made out of old pink shoelaces. She and her best friend Mary would meet at their clubhouse next to the old barn in Ruthie's back yard. Ruthie would carefully take the necklace off her neck and unlock the door. Then she'd put the necklace back on and the two girls would run inside and plop down on a big yellow pillow they used as a couch.

Mary would open up her backpack and pull out their favorite chocolate chip cookies that her mother had made. Together the girls would eat cookies and giggle. They each kept a doll at the clubhouse, and once the cookies were gone they played with their dolls. Most of all they giggled – they loved to giggle.

When it was time to leave, they'd put the dolls in pajamas and tuck them into the bed that they'd made out of an old apple basket. Each doll had a special blanket that had been cut from a soft blue and white beach towel. When the dolls were in bed, the girls would tidy up the club house, still giggling, and then head outside. Ruthie would once again remove the pink necklace and use the key to lock up their special clubhouse.

As you can see, using a prompt is key to unlocking creative thinking.

Prompt: **Low Tide**   May 14, 2014
Marilyn Page

I have no idea why the prompt "Low Tide" came to mind this morning. I suppose if I stopped and thought for a minute or two and reflected on the early morning, I'd understand.

You see, with my coffee mug in hand, the dog and I went to our usual spot to look out the back window. It was only 5:00 a.m. but already the red fox was making its way up the path through the field. Behind it was the Bay – peaceful as the tide had settled low.

I never cease to marvel at God's creation: blue herons lazily wading through the mud looking for something tasty to eat, ducks paddling around in only inches of water, and the cormorants standing proudly on the tops of rocks that jut upward from the mud.

Low Tide can at first sound negative, but I find it a wonderful term. Sure, it's always fun when the tide is high and the water welcomes us to swim or boat or simply play. Yet low tide calls us to ponder peace, to look for a deeper beauty in things around us.

I'm glad low tide came to my mind. It's a reminder for me to look at the positives in my life, to see my glass as more than half full, never empty.

Low Tide...it makes my spirit high.

Prompt: **Sounds**   Oct. 28, 2014
Marilyn Page

The mist was finally starting to disappear, as Jo-Anne and I sat in our beach chairs with our towels wrapped around us. Until now we had only heard the voices of fellow beach lovers. As the sun was burning through that mist, we began to see people, lots of people.

It seemed that as the sun got brighter the sounds intensified. Even the seagulls were louder than usual, perhaps trying to out-shout the high-pitched happy voices of the kids. And kids were everywhere. It's a happy sound when kids are having a great adventure, whether building sand castles or playing in the water. The sound of a voice can often say more than the words spoken. On this day, it was about pure happiness. And it made me happy too!

How nice to think that our voices, the tone and cadence of them, can put a smile on someone's face. Sure the words are important, but without the right voice the words can lose their meaning.

At the beach, listening to children play with complete abandonment, words were not important. Their excitement couldn't be expressed with a thousand words. Their simple squeals of laughter spilled over to my listening ear, calling me to break away from the mist and enjoy life to the fullest.

Prompt: **Three Old Ladies**   June 9, 2015
Marilyn Page

There they were again, walking arm-in-arm along Main Street. The only time they let go of each other was to stop and discuss an item on display in a store window. Somehow they always ended up giggling before taking up their position of arm-in-arm as they continued walking through the center of town. Good thing it was a pedestrian only area.

I don't know how long these three old ladies had been together, but my guess was that they were life-long friends.

I first noticed them about a year ago. I'd started coming into the town center with a guide dog puppy I was training. I came almost every Wednesday, and so did they.

Many times I wanted to talk with them, but somehow it didn't seem right for me to break in on their special time together. So I simply enjoyed them from a distance. Until the day the woman on the left noticed me and my black puppy with his yellow jacket. She said something to her friends, pointed to me and before I knew it they were standing in front of me.

"We hope we're not bothering you," one of them said. "We've seen you here almost every Wednesday with your puppy. We've wanted to talk with you, to ask you about your puppy, but we could tell you were busy and we didn't want to intrude."

"Intrude!" I exclaimed. "Not at all. I've been wanting to meet all of you too."

For the next hour or so my puppy and I had a delightful time chatting with the three old ladies, enjoying our new friendship and giggling even as we said, "See you next Wednesday!"

Prompt: **Lying in the Gutter**   June 13, 2015
Marilyn Page

Her mind went blank. She could think of nothing coherent, only bits and pieces of the many great stories that had just been shared from the delightful group of writers at Norm's Round Table. The writing prompt that had just been given wasn't working, so she tossed it aside and left it 'Lying in the Gutter.' It simply didn't fit.

What did fit were thoughts of how enjoyable the writing year had been. The group is diverse; each writer creative in their own unique way. Some write poems, some write memoirs, others create amazing stories. They listen, laugh, critique and beg for more.

There's no pressure at the Round Table. It's a time to relax, when stories and adventures are written and shared.

This writer is glad she left the prompt 'Lying in the Gutter', and used the time instead to tell her *Round Table* friends, "Thanks for your writing; have a good summer."

Prompt: **The Orange Coffin**   May 10, 2015
Barbie LaMarca

"Coffins are boring" proclaimed Melba. "When I die, I don't want to be boxed forever in a shellacked tube or an impermeable metal vault."

Mouths dropped around the table accompanied by gasps and groans. Mitchell warned, "Mother, we are eating dinner. That is a totally inappropriate topic!"

"We're all gonna die — it's a fact of life. I'm likely closer to the inevitable than the rest of you; it's on my mind a lot these days. Since all the people I love are sitting at this table, what better time to express my final wishes?"

Polly piped in, "Mummy, you are only seventy-eight years old. I'm sure we'll be blessed to have you another twenty years, at least."

"Or cursed," muttered Jason under his breath.

"Maybe, maybe not. In the meantime, I would like to design my own coffin and have it built by a talented craftsman."

"What about cremation?" Alan asked.

"Go up in a heap of fiery blaze!? I don't like that idea one little bit! No way! I've been pondering it for many days and I've written it all down. This is what I'd like.

"My coffin will be orange with white trim like a Creamsicle, which is my favorite ice cream treat. It will be lined with silk and rabbit's fur, which are two of the softest materials I'd want to be wrapped in. I want an exterior bell on a toggle string attached to the inside of the coffin just in case there's been a mistake and I want to get out.

"I'm to be dressed in a black negligee, so I'll look sexy when I run into Mr. Wonderful on the other side.

"Any questions?"

Everyone was too stunned to utter a word.

Prompt: **It All Ends Tomorrow**   Mar. 6, 2012
Barbie LaMarca

Eleanor surveyed the multitude of packed boxes surrounding her. Labels of "crystal," "knick knacks," "books," "photo albums," "flatware," and "china" were made with black markers. A life was in those boxes — the life she shared with Harvey until he died two years ago.

She remembered the evening in the park when this awkward young man tripped over her because he was looking up at a stunning full moon. As the apologetic words tumbled out of his mouth, their eyes met and something magical happened.

Their ethnic backgrounds and social circles were very different, but they built a relationship from shared likes, reasonable compromises, and an irrepressible chemistry. The void experienced when apart could not be filled by others.

The wedding had been a simple ceremony in the chapel on the top of Mt. Casper. They honeymooned in a log cabin by the lake. Nine months later, Jacob was born. Two years passed and Abigail arrived. By their tenth anniversary, they were proud parents also of Ethan and Marie. Typical of life, there were struggles — physical and financial challenges. But, the river of their love and faith ran strong beneath their feet.

She thought of the time Ethan fell through the ice. It was the frantic barking of George, the stray mutt Ethan had brought home one day, which brought Eleanor's attention to the mishap. This memory made her reflect on the notions of destiny versus coincidence and she decided that everything that had happened in her life was meant to be.

And so, now, at the age of 89, it was time to leave many of the physical treasures of her very full life behind. She was disabled to the point of needing constant care. Marie had added a small apartment to her home in the country. The four children had set up an account to fund a full-time nurse.

Tomorrow — the disconnect from the tactile reminders of her past. However, the past was preserved in her memories. Jacob would wheel her from one phase of her life into the new one about to begin.

Prompt: **The Silent World**   Feb. 5, 2013
Barbie LaMarca

In silence —
The sun rises,
A constant and
Welcome event,
Assuring a new day.

In silence —
Butterflies move
Through the air,
Pheromones
Communicating.

In silence —
The deaf/mute girl
Processes her environment,
Calculates
Her response to it.

In silence —
A glider soars
On air currents,
Drifting, descending,
Glancing the earth on landing.

In silence —
Snow swirls,
Floats,
Blankets the earth.

In silence —
Clouds roll,
Forming and
Reforming shapes,
Whatever the eye perceives.

In silence —
The embryo
Develops,
Becomes a specialized
Living being.

In silence —
Judgments form,
Unspoken,
Destructive,
Hatred brews.

In silence —
A child feels love
As mother cradles him,
Rocks him
To sleep.

In silence —
The sun sets,
Reminding us
That all things
Have a beginning, and an end.

Prompt: **The Clock Winked**   Feb. 14, 2012
Barbie LaMarca

Giuseppe's eyes were tired. He'd been painstakingly cleaning the works of a remarkable old clock. The mechanism was comprised of the tiniest gears he had ever seen.

It had been brought to the shop by an ugly old crone. She introduced herself as Bethelda. When she handed the mahogany cased clock to him, she said it was imperative that the clock be fixed by the eve of the winter solstice. Giuseppe asked her about the origin of the clock. She glared at him with dark, beady eyes, and said that it was none of his concern. "It is very ancient and has mystical powers," she barked.

She did not know how long it had been dormant, but it was time for it to wake up. When it didn't stir, she wondered if the gears might be rusted. She had heard that Giuseppe was the best with all types of timepieces.

"I'll be back in four days. If it is running, you will be handsomely rewarded."

The little clock was quite unique – its face actually looked like the face of a Buddha with bulbous cheeks and slanted eyes. There were symbols in place of numbers for the hours. He did not recognize them.

While he gingerly reconstructed its inner self, each time he correctly placed a gear he thought he heard a giggle. "I must be getting too old for this – I am hearing things. I must make some time for the company of human beings instead of clocks."

Finally, at the 11th hour of the 4th day, the last piece was placed and he closed the casing. When he turned the clock around, it winked at him. "Now, I am seeing things!"

Several minutes before midnight, the old crone appeared. She took the clock from him without a word and turned to face the moon beyond the window. She held out the clock, muttered a few words, and they both disappeared.

In a state of shock, Giuseppe turned to sit down and noticed a small brown pouch on his workbench. When he opened it, there were twelve sparkling diamonds inside – one for each hour of the clock.

Prompt: **Paper Airplanes**   Mar. 25, 2014
Barbie LaMarca

Mrs. Kemplar was called to the office at 10:15 a.m. She had just passed out math worksheets to her fourth-grade students.

"Please remain in your seats and work on your math problems until I return. Amy, please write the names of any students who talk or get out of their seats."

Henry sat by the windows and was watching the contrail of a passing jet against the deep teal sky. As he daydreamed of being the pilot in that plane, he took his worksheet and folded it to aerodynamic standards and let it soar across the room. It landed on Peter's desk.

At first, Peter was startled and was about to shout, "Hey, who threw this?" when he remembered that Amy was taking names. So, he took his worksheet and whipped up a sleek version of the F-111 that his daddy told stories about, then let it fly.

It landed on Jimmy's desk and he thought, "What a great idea!" His worksheet plane landed on Shirley's desk.

Shirley hated math and had been stuck on a division problem. She took her sheet and designed her own plane. Hers landed in the trash can with a thunk.

By this point, all of the students, except Frank — who loved math and was totally absorbed in his work — were making and flying planes. A couple of them landed on Mrs. Kemplar's desk, and before their creators could retrieve them, the door opened and there she stood.

The kids held their breath as Cassie's plane was mid-air and heading right for their teacher's hair. Mrs. Kemplar looked around the room slowly, as she made her way to her desk after feeling the soft crunch on her head.

Amy's hand shot up, but she didn't wait to be called and squealed, "Nobody talked and no one got out of their seats, Mrs. Kemplar!"

The teacher wanted to chuckle but stifled the urge. Instead, she took two pieces of paper and crafted an adorable bi-wing, released it, and watched it soar — along with sixteen other little heads — to the back of the room.

First one, then another, stunned student started to giggle.

"It's a beautiful day. Grab your planes and we'll go outside and fly them!"

The news in the office had been very sad, but the behavior of the students somehow lifted her spirits, along with the paper airplanes, toward the sky.

Prompt: **Ode to Springtime in New Hampshire**   May 19, 2015
Ted King

While motoring into Exeter earlier on this fine spring morning, I chanced to spot a storage facility alongside the Brentwood Road, in front of which a large purple lilac was in full bloom. That got me thinking that New Hampshire is represented by the purple lilac. It's the state flower!

I know of no sweeter aroma than that of the lilac. Just two days ago I was stopped dead in my tracks, on my daily perambulation of our neighborhood, by that lovely lilac scent. As I rounded the corner onto my street, I spotted the source of that perfumed aroma: Mark and Trillium's white lilac blooming profusely and proudly.

Last week my New Hampshire raised spouse, Margaret, surprised me by having our own backyard purple lilacs, growing within our perennial garden, physically uprooted and dragged away by our lawn-garden-tree expert-and-helper, Mark. She claimed that our lilac variety was an inferior, pathetic bloomer and wasn't worth the space they grew on.

The good news is that our back yard is yet to come into its full blooming glory within the next two weeks. More specifically, on Memorial Day weekend the festival of blooming woodsy shrubs of all kinds, largely rhododendrons and azaleas, will more than make up for those few, absent, forlorn lilacs!

Prompt: **There Was This Photograph**   Nov. 3, 2015
Ted King

Florence Hart Frost, my maternal grandmother known to us grandchildren as Nanna, like her daughter, Janet Frost King, my mother, was a habitual worrier about having her photograph taken. For whatever reason, both women didn't care for the way their likenesses appeared. Late in Nanna's life, she would pre-plan her poses. My mother, also, I noticed, tended to stand up straighter, tuck her chin in, and suck in her waist. Certainly, these were the obvious and simplest ways to help improve one's photogenic looks, short of cosmetic surgery!

Nanna liked the color blue. As did many others of her "dandelion headed" (as she referred to them) female crowd in their eighties at her Cleveland, Ohio retirement home, she tinted her white hair with a touch of blue!

While in medical school a few blocks away, I received a photo of Nanna, personalized as follows: "From Nanna, 85, to Ted, 25." She was posing beside her prized collection of rare blue and white demitasse cups on display at her Wade Park Manor home. What a thoughtful gift: my favorite grandmother's photo of herself, sitting beside her own favorite things, for one of her favorite grandsons!

Prompt: **In an Instant**   Oct. 16, 2015
Ted King

My "new normal," following that fell stroke of 2003, over a dozen years ago, left me with severe left hemiplegia. In spite of the difficult early years following that nearly fatal injury, now it amazes me how much better my life has become despite the stroke!

What a change in my attitude this is from my initial astonishment that my body could so disappoint me, after having gotten me through so many previous tight spots. At first after that stroke, I would often curse myself over my inability to accomplish a simple daily chore, such as donning a tee shirt.

On the other hand, I am now greatly pleased that I've been freed from having to carry a beeper while "on call' to the hospital. Perhaps that beeper stressor alone caused the stroke in the first place!

Pre-stroke, my young colleagues at work made it clear to me and other partners my age that they would not be eager to allow us to slow down gradually – winding down our practices as we entered our well-deserved retirements.

This stroke of mine, however, put me into sudden retirement in an instant – unquestionably, totally, permanently, and guilt free on my behalf! Far from remaining disappointed with this 69 year-old body of mine, I'm now looking forward to what the future has in store.

Most of all, I'm so pleased that I didn't die during those nip and tuck early post stroke days in the intensive care units of both Exeter Hospital and the Lahey Clinic, in Burlington, Massachusetts.

Although this storm crossed my path, I believe my life was saved for a purpose.

Prompt: **Mickey Won the Race**   Mar. 22, 2016
Ted King

Desiring to win any race in which I'm a contestant must be an inherent element of my DNA. That is one of the many things I've learned about myself since a serious stroke "took most of the wind from my sails," so to speak, exactly 13 years ago tomorrow, on March 23, 2003. Since then I've been living with left hemiplegia – spastic, numb, and uncoordinated left arm and left leg.

Regaining my lost physical skills and coordination, is one thing. But I'm eager to prove that I'm no beginner in any of those pre-stroke sports in which I once was competitive. Whether it's downhill skiing or "round the buoys" sailboat racing, I enter any contest to win it!

As a consistent winner before the stroke, of all three (gold, silver, or bronze) NASTAR downhill timed slalom ski races, I feel sufficient confidence in my current abilities in skiing to regain similar prizes, perhaps even during this season if the spring snow holds out!

However, whatever the results, no matter where I am, whether on skis or in a sailboat, I hope to be able to say – as did the apostle Paul in 2 Timothy 4:7 – that in spite of great adversity "I have fought the good fight, I have finished the race, I have kept the faith."

Ultimately, the real victory for me is persevering under trial and standing the test to receive the crown of life that the Lord promised to those who love Him (James 1:12).

Prompt: **She Had Drifted for Days**   Mar. 1, 2016
Ted King

From my first ocean sailing race, aboard the 70-foot wooden schooner, "Nina," skippered by the venerable former New York Yacht Club Commodore DeCoursey Fales, in the 1963 Storm Trysail Club's Block Island Race, to my most recent major offshore ocean race 37 years later, aboard another former New York Yacht Club Commodore Frank V. Snyder's, Ted Hood designed Little Harbor 54-foot "Chasseur" in the 2000 millennial year Newport to Bermuda Race, I've been impressed, nearly every time, with how fickle the winds can be, even hundreds of miles out to sea. Also, given any steady breeze, it's not unusual to witness marked changes in velocity, whether up or down, and changes in direction. These changes often occur within minutes.

Many is the race I've finished, in what might later be spoken of, due to extremely light breezes, as a "drifting match!"

The most memorable "drifting match" I recall was the 1973 Fastnet Race, in which I served as a watch captain among the crew. I was aboard a different "Chasseur," a brand new Sparkman & Stephens designed Swan 44-foot ocean racing vessel which Frank Snyder had custom built and recently launched in Finland. After his family sailed "Chasseur" with him from Finland to England, Frank's trusty racing crew replaced his family to learn the ropes and practice racing at Cowes Race Week, prior to racing to Ireland in the legendary Fastnet Race.

We raced a total of over 600 nautical miles from Cowes, on the Isle of Wight on England's southern coast, crossing the Celtic Sea, rounding the Fastnet Rock Island Lighthouse off the most southerly point of Ireland, turning 180 degrees back toward Plymouth, passing south of the Scilly Isles forty-five miles off Land's End of the Cornwall coast, and finishing at the breakwater at Plymouth Harbor. Taking several days longer than expected, this may have been the slowest Fastnet Race in history, which is a notoriously challenging and often dangerous race due to gale force winds. In this race, that was not the case!

Following an uneventful westbound leg, in normal ocean airs, after rounding the craggy outcropping of Fastnet Rock, it was during our homeward leg, returning to England, that we experienced something of a "sea change." Plagued by very soft wind conditions, we just barely moved forward, ghosting along, with sails flat, and no sea motion. At other times we became marooned in a dead flat calm. Aimless hours stretched into perhaps three more days, to gain the inland harbor of Plymouth.

I recall most vividly drifting toward the finish line, within a boat length or so, of Prime Minister Sir Edward Heath's shiny new wooden sloop "Morning Cloud." A powerful Offshore Patrol motor launch approached carrying official photographers. In hushed, polite tones, we heard the commanding officer hailing the Prime Minister with the following: "Begging your pardon, Mr. Prime Minister Sir, you have an errant, untidy line (rope) hanging overboard, which might not look good in the photos!" We watched closely, as a crew member scampered to retrieve that vagrant length of line, and return it to its rightful place, aboard, just before the finishing signal sounded.

Post Script

It's significant to me that both my first and my final offshore ocean sailing races were aboard well-known ocean racing yachts, "Nina" and "Chasseur." Both vessels were captained by their renowned owners, New York Yacht Club Commodores DeCoursey Fales and Frank Snyder.

My then 20-year-old son, Robbie, was aboard "Chasseur" with me in 2000. This was my 15th and Robbie's second Newport to Bermuda Race. This race was to be Frank's last. He died suddenly in 2006 at his summer home on Martha's Vineyard, Massachusetts, while preparing for a race.

Prompt: **She Had Drifted for Days**   Mar. 1, 2016
Don Nolte

It began as an ambitious, self-powered trip across the channel, to prove something. She had a motor on her little craft, just as backup, and even an extra pair of oars. She was a planner.

But the best plans suffer a well-known though seldom heeded fate. The storm that nearly washed her overboard disposed of the extra oars, and most of her supplies – and when it dawned on her, after too many dawns, that she wasn't going to make it on her own power, she cranked the little motor, and cranked, and cranked, and cranked, and finally gave up.

How to get the small outboard going was beyond her ken, and despite her planning she had no radio, not even a GPS. The sun was reliable in pointing East, but it was also a reliable source of heat, adding to the irritation of her hunger and thirst.

She had been on a diet, to lose a few pounds, but this went too far. Her mind began to wander. Surely a ship must come by, but no. A lazy shark cruised past, seemingly uninterested in her meagerness.

A drifter, she thought, a wanderer, a soul seeking the meaning of life, a spot in timelessness. Would she be found, would she cast up on a warm and friendly beach, would she be responsive enough to know, or care? Would she be alive?

Her friends had suggested this venture might not be advisable, but advisableness and prudence had not placed high in her priorities of life. She had been politically involved in seeking ways to advance women's issues, and had come to think one way was to show women were as resourceful as men.

Now she felt the uniformness of humanity, the minuteness of each man or woman before the expanse of the cosmos. If there were a God, she might soon meet her.

Now, sensing her humanity, she reflected upon the literature of philosophy, the Rhyme of the Ancient Mariner, her youthful fascination with science fiction, her own attempts at composition and poetry, the loves of her life, her feelings of warmth as a child in a sheltered home, the musical strains of Chopin, Bach, Sibelius.

She wondered where it all would end, as she drifted into sleep.

Prompt: **Storm's Coming**   Mar. 15, 2016
Don Nolte

James Eldon Cagley sat on his porch. Not again, he thought – some weeks ago they had nearly been flooded away.

Their house was a raised ranch, about seventy-five years old; they were the third or fourth owners. Nancy, his wife, was not particularly keen on this place, seeing it as merely a stepping stone on the path of life. "Any port in a storm," she had been heard to say.

Husband Jim was a bit happier with the place, working every weekend to fix it up, not just to flip it for some profit in a year or two, but with some notion that it might be a place to hold onto, rent out, and return to one day.

The challenge at the moment was to make whatever preparations he could for the approaching weather pattern. The Weather Service had gotten better at predicting what "actually might happen" – his favorite sort of forecast was "50% chance of" (whatever they announced). This time it was a Nor'easter that could be seen on all the radar maps, not much question about this one.

Their cellar had seen a lot of ground water over the years; he had installed not only one but two sump pumps. Water came to them down a gentle slope from neighbors up the street, and he had channeled it with a swale to go further down the block, and had tied in drainage tubes from the house's downspouts. His downhill neighbors loved him for this.

With this drainage system and pretty good storm windows he wasn't really worried, yet there was something primordial about the feelings such weather predictions occasioned. He wondered how high the winds would be, and how they might impact tall trees not far from the house. They had insurance, of course, but one couldn't help being concerned.

They wondered if it would behoove them to batten the hatches, hop in the car, and head for some safer location. But inertia won the day.

James Eldon Cagley had a choice to make,
Whether to hunker down, or to seek a clean break.
His wife was likely to insist on leaving town,
Despite her certainty that James would merely frown.
Hopefully, no argument would cloud their wedded bliss,
And hopefully, when all was done, naught would be amiss.
James finished his tasks and grabbed his TV Guide,
The missus opened a book and put her cares aside.
The two would cope, each in their own way,
As curiously they wondered what would come this day.

Prompt: **Down the Cobblestone Alley**   Mar. 22, 2016
Don Nolte

It was a touristy part of town. They came from Europe, from South America, most recently from China and elsewhere in the Orient.

The tour books and web sites hyped this neighborhood as a place to gain a sense of how the famous author lived, surely in hopes of coming to understand how she encountered the world, and thus to see how she developed her deep, perceptive *Weltanschauung*, her inimitable world view.

Of course the local merchants, book sellers and restaurateurs cared only for the value added to their product by this mystique. Most of them had not even read her works. They knew enough from perusing news articles to converse with tourists and pretend to know more than they did. Especially the inn-keepers.

To them, the dreamers and seekers were merely wandering down a primrose path, this cobblestone alley, this yellow brick road. The visitors were looking for something, and if the merchants could manage it, they were intent on helping them think they had found it.

The jaded locals knew that in life the notion that we have embraced eternal truths is about as much as we can hope for, the belief that we have found what we are seeking – whether one might actually find it remains an open question, as we journey down the cobblestone alley of life.

Prompt: **What about Charlie?**   Mar. 8, 2016
Ursula Nolte

We were sitting in the living room listening to music.

Looking out of the window was a wonderful sight. It was spring; all the snow had melted. The green tips of the growing leaves were already visible. We could hear the birds chirping.

The little chipmunk had just come out of its hole and nibbled on the seeds we recently put out in the feeder near the ground. It was warm enough that the windows could be opened to let the fresh air in.

There was a lot of activity going on outside now. The squirrels were chasing each other around the trees. Throughout the year we had been watching them and we had given them names for their individual features.

We recognized Freda, Otto, and Ida. But what about Charlie, the red squirrel? We had not seen him in a while. Where was he hiding? He always had been the first at the feeder. We wondered what happened to him. Was he killed by a coyote or a bobcat?

Suddenly there was something moving and jumping up to the birdfeeder at the window outside. There he was, peeking with his curious little eyes into the living room and munching on the seeds. We were very relieved and happy to have him back.

Prompt: **Storm's Coming**   Mar. 15, 2016
Ursula Nolte

They went out in their fishing boat. It was a hot day. The sun's rays burned their wrinkled faces and sweat ran down their cheeks. The sea was calm, its surface glittering like silver. It was a beautiful sight. Fish were nearing the surface. It looked promising for a great catch.

But far, far in the distance lurked a small white cloud. It came nearer and nearer and grew larger and larger. While working frantically to catch as many fish as they could, they did not pay attention to the weather until the whole sky was filled with clouds and turned darker and darker.

As they became aware of the approaching storm, waves splashed against the boat and it shook. Water came over the sides. Hurriedly they lowered the sail. Now the storm arrived in full power.

Thunder and lightning surrounded them and tormented them in their small boat. Their lives were in danger. They realized their helplessness against the power of the storm and had to wait it out.

After a while the sea became calm again. As the boat drifted slowly, they sighed in relief.

Looking at the fish they had caught that day, they were satisfied. It was a dangerous life, exposed to the power of the sea, but somehow they loved it and knew that they would go out again and again. It was their way.

Prompt: **Down the Cobblestone Alley**   Mar. 22, 2016
Ursula Nolte

During the war, bombs were falling around us in the city, and it was recommended by the government that mothers and children should be evacuated to the countryside and small towns.

Neighbors decided to get together, three women and four kids, to take the train to a little town north of Frankfurt am Main.

We departed in the early afternoon, but the little train had to stop midway to wait until the noise of enemy airplanes above us was not heard anymore. Then we could continue with our travel.

It was night and quite dark when we reached the small town of our destination. The friendly relative of our neighbor came with her hand pulled rack-wagon to receive us at the railroad station.

Our few belongings were piled on the wagon and off it went, rattling down the cobblestone alley. My mother walked behind, worried that something might fall off.

While keeping a close eye on the ground, she saw a dark object. Thinking it might have fallen from the wagon, she reached down to pick it up. To her great surprise, it felt soft – she was holding a cow pie.

A farmer must have been there earlier with his cow-drawn wagon, to deliver milk or other products, and left his mark. That was our first encounter as city people with the countryside, where we would stay to wait out the end of the war.

Prompt: All the Lights Went Out and ...   May 10, 2016
Ursula Nolte

It was after we heard the sirens going to signal the approach of enemy airplanes. We lived at the time in a first-floor apartment in a suburb of Frankfurt (Main).

The people from the second and third floor rushed with us, with our gas masks, into the basement, where a small community room had been designated as our bomb shelter. Here we huddled together, awaiting what was coming – three women with three children, and one man in uniform.

One of the children was very sick; she had a heart defect and was blue all over. The man was home on leave from the military, the other fathers were somewhere at the front.

When the sirens stopped, it became quiet in the room. All of a sudden there was an explosion; we heard bricks falling through the chimney, and the lights went out. The sick girl whimpered, and not only the children cried out.

But with all this noise, the voice of the man in uniform was heard saying: "Don't be such sissies, this occurs for the future of our *Reich* and we must endure it." My mother was very upset about this statement and aired her anger with some remarks that I cannot specifically recall.

The sirens came on again, this time to signal the end of the air raid, and we all stumbled silently upstairs to our apartments, relieved that we were still alive.

The next morning we saw that we had barely escaped the destruction of our building; a bomb had hit the house just behind us. A few days later we were evacuated to the countryside, where we stayed until the end of the war.

Section 3

Selected Writings by

Writers of the Round Table

Ticonderoga
Norman Phillips

There's something I like about sharpening a pencil with a pocket knife. I don't think too much about it, but often, in the quiet room where I sit and write, memories of my grandfather blossom when I start to sharpen a pencil. I can almost feel the warm glow of the wood-burning stove where on cold days he sat and taught me to use his pocket knife. I see him sitting by the stove, leaning over the wood box, his strong hands holding a pencil that he never learned to use, his thumb pressing the back of a sharp blade as he sliced a golden chip from the end of my Ticonderoga pencil.

I remember coming home from the first or second grade and being greeted in the kitchen by my grandparents. "Here comes the little scholar!" my grandfather said cheerfully.

He was an illiterate Polish immigrant and didn't speak English, but I could tell by the sound of his voice that he was proud of his grandson who was learning to write. Each day I came home from school he'd take my pencil box over to his chair next to the stove and wood box, sit down and take out his pocket knife and start to sharpen my pencil. Like most little boys, I was intrigued by his knife. It had a brown bone handle that was partly broken on one side, revealing a rivet. The knife had two blades. One of them was long and worn thin from countless sharpening over many years. The smaller blade, the one he used for my pencils, he kept razor-sharp. He beckoned me closer and examined the small blade, running his finger along the edge. He'd glance my way with a twinkle in his eye and he'd say, "Dobrze!" (Good!) and then he'd select a pencil that I'd worn down or broken. Grandpa examined the pencil carefully and made sure I was watching him. He held the knife in his right hand and the pencil in his left and then with the thumb of his left hand he pushed the blade smoothly into the yellow wood. The chip curled up and dropped into the wood box. He did this slowly with a serious look on his wrinkled face. It became a ritual that I looked forward to every day after school. I knew that my grandpa respected and approved of my school work and I began to feel more important and a little less the child that I was.

At school we were shown how to use the pencil sharpener, screwed into the wood molding surrounding the blackboard. It had a handle that you turned while holding the pencil tightly after you inserted it into the hole. The cover of the sharpener was taken off after it was filled with the crinkly pairings and we got to empty it into the teacher's wastebasket. I never could figure out how the spiral grooves of the mechanism sharpened the pencil but it did and the pencils came away with a smooth and sharp point. I liked grandpa's sharpening better. You could see where each chip was cut off and the lead that was bared was thicker and didn't break off when you pressed the pencil down hard. I always broke my point when I used the sharpener at school. When you're cranking the sharpener you can look around and make faces at your classmates. Of course, it's easy to see why a teacher can't have young students whittling away at their pencils with sharp knives. The school nurse would probably run out of Band-Aids! Besides, nowadays, pocket knives are considered weapons. But at home, under the watchful eye of my grandpa, I was eventually handed his knife and guided into the craft of pencil sharpening. Grandpa held my small hands in his, and together we cut my first pencil. He showed me how to push the blade smoothly with the thumb of the hand that held the pencil, and he showed me what happens when you try to slash it with the other hand. Almost every time, the lead would break off and the pencil became shorter and shorter. Grandpa was a frugal man, and he couldn't bear to see a pencil cut short by inept sharpening, and at the same time, he was tenderly training me to not cut my young fingers.

After many weeks, I was allowed to use grandpa's knife by myself. Of course, he was always there looking over my shoulder, and I earnestly tried to win his approving nod. And then one day, after I'd sharpened all my pencils, he took the knife out of my hands, folded the short blade and open the long one and began to peel an apple. I was mesmerized by the jiggling, unbroken spiral of apple peel that he deftly sliced away until the naked apple was exposed. He cut off a large piece, speared it with the blade and offered it to me. I knew right then that I had won his approval! Grandpa then told me that whenever I needed to sharpen my pencil, I could use his knife.

And so it was that I grew to love the feel of a sharp blade smoothly paring away the yellow chip of my Ticonderoga. It has become a ritual for me. I now keep a handful of pencils in a ceramic jar along with an old black pocket knife. The knife rests there waiting, in the midst of its dependent companions.

These days when I go to an office supply store, I see a great variety of mechanical devices that sharpen pencils. I suppose they're used in offices, schools and even at home. It seems to me that pocket knives aren't used as much as they used to be. When I was a boy I think we carried one, but now...

I saunter by a long display of writing implements – pens – pencils – markers – there must be at least 100 choices! There are countless mechanical pencils and packets of lead to fill them. There are at least a half-dozen different kinds of electric pencil sharpeners displayed and numerous sharpeners that you can turn with a handle and others that can be twisted around the point of the pencil. And yes, at the end of the display, where you hardly notice them, there are a few of the old-fashioned, yellow, six sided wooden pencils.

It makes me think. I can't imagine writing with something other than the pencil – a wooden pencil. Somehow it connects me to my childhood, my school days and my grandpa who showed me how to sharpen my Ticonderoga pencils with his pocket knife.

The Ice Cream Trail
David Johnson

The most noticeable feature about Veteran, Wyoming is its lack of features. The town, so named because of the number of WWI veterans who settled there, consists of a post office, a small general store, a school and a nondescript collection of houses and outbuildings. Unlike many parts of Wyoming where rugged desolation creates beauty, Veteran is just forlorn. Summers are hot, dry and windy with temperatures often exceeding 100 degrees. Winters are cold with nothing to stop the wind from any direction. Hardy farmers who throw fate to the wind in this part of Wyoming are at the mercy of Mother Nature. Farmers who made it through the dust bowl of the 30's raised frugality to an art form, and my Grandfather Eaton was their imam. It's no wonder he decided to invest some of his hard-earned money on a winter home in Southern California once the next generation was capable of manning the farm.

Granddad's call came as a surprise. Knowing he probably had the first nickel ever to grace his pocket, I couldn't understand why he would waste it on a long-distance call to me. This was a man who mandated that my grandmother extend scrambled eggs with soda crackers; he kept my mom out of school until the fifth grade so she could help him on the farm, and he installed cost-cutting fluorescent lights in the living room of his house, long before they were in vogue. Whatever he had to say must have been very important. When I heard his voice crackle over the party line asking, "Would you be willing to fly to California and drive Grandma and me back to Wyoming for the summer?" I could barely contain my excitement. As I pondered who would pay for the airfare, he said, "I'll pay for your plane ticket from Denver to Los Angeles, just try to keep the cost down." His parting comment was, "There's a bus from Los Angeles to Riverside. I'll meet you at the station."

So began my great adventure.

I grew up in Wyoming, but far removed from Veteran's featureless plain. My father's family homesteaded near Laramie in the late 1800's. The ranch is at the base of a mountain with a mile of the Big Laramie River running through it. The mountain, the river and the groves of aspen and cottonwood trees, provided a beautiful backdrop for my childhood years. Despite its natural beauty the ranch was quiet and, by the time I graduated from high school, I had more than a little wanderlust to see what lay beyond Wyoming's borders. In June of 1970, I had just turned nineteen and had just finished my freshman year at the University of Wyoming. Granddad's offer was just what the doctor ordered.

The excitement was palpable as I thought of my first airplane trip followed by a driving adventure with two senior citizens. All I had to do was get to Denver, a three-hour drive away. I prevailed on some friends who agreed to take me to the airport in exchange for gas money. Granddad's parting words to "keep the cost down" were echoing in my mind as I walked into Stapleton International Airport. The United Airlines ticket agent was not only competent, but she was nice and pretty, and she didn't seem to notice that I was out of my element as I stood at the counter shaking hayseeds from my sunburned ears. With my University of Wyoming student ID and $30.00 I was in possession of an economy class standby ticket to LA.

My seatmate was a young woman who had the demeanor of a well-seasoned traveler. Of course, relative to me, probably everyone on the plane was a well-seasoned traveler! Not wanting to appear the country rube I was, I regaled her of my travel experiences. Sharing the details of a family trip to Omaha in a 1961 Plymouth was probably not the best way to impress this woman. In fact, it was probably the final blow to our budding friendship as she rapidly lost interest in me. Fortunately, my attention was turned to the free food and drink offered by the flight attendant. I could get used to this.

As the plane began its descent into Los Angeles I pressed my face to the window, taking in the urban sprawl that lay below. My father's cousin, an escapee of the Wyoming cold who lived in Redondo Beach, met me at the airport and chauffeured me to the downtown bus station for my trip to Riverside.

As the bus pulled into Riverside I saw Granddad's old beige Dodge Coronet. He stood leaning against the car watching the passengers step from the bus. It wasn't until I was a few feet from him and said, "Hi Granddad" that he recognized me. He hadn't seen me for a year or so but I thought it odd he didn't recognize me. Once he got behind the wheel of the old Dodge and started to drive I realized why.

"Is that light red or green?" he asked as we sat at an intersection near the bus station. I said, "It's red," to which he responded, "Well, tell me when it turns green."

Granddad was virtually blind! Now I understood why I had been tapped to drive him and Grandma back to Wyoming. We didn't say much on the way to the house. What little talking there was consisted of, "Is there a light here?" "Yes," "What color is it?" "It's red," "What color is it now?" "It's still red but it's getting ready to change," "It's green," "There's a stop sign ahead!" "No there isn't, there's never been a stop sign here," "Well, it's there now and it's red with eight sides!!!" "Ok, if you say so, where do I stop?" "Right here!" and he slammed on the brakes. I wondered how many times he had run the stop sign before I alerted him to its existence. I also wondered how he had found the bus station in the first place.

As we pulled into the driveway I couldn't help but contrast my grandparent's California house to their farmhouse in Veteran. The house was a small bungalow, just the right size for two people. Granddad satisfied his farming urges by growing roses and the front yard was full of blossoming bushes of every size and color. On one side of the house was an orange grove with what appeared to be ripe fruit on the trees. Grandma Eaton met me at the door. She provided a perfect counterpoint to Granddad's flinty edginess for she was as kind and gentle as a woman could be. She showed me to my room and said, "Make yourself at home, dinner will be ready in a few minutes." My last meal had been served at 36,000 feet and I was ravenous. After dinner, Granddad asked if I'd like some ice cream for dessert. If Granddad had a sweet spot, it was ice cream.

After breakfast the following morning, Granddad told me the plan for our upcoming journey.

"We're going to be pulling a trailer to Wyoming this year," he stated. "Ice cream is expensive in Wyoming. It's 59¢ for a half gallon there and I can buy a half gallon here for only 39¢ so we're going to take a freezer full of ice cream back with us."

The fact that we were driving across the desert with a freezer full of ice cream in June when the temperatures can exceed 100 degrees seemed odd, but then, who was I to question? This was just another part of the adventure. We went to the carport where the trailer was parked. Granddad would only drive cars made by Chrysler, but in the truck department, he was a Studebaker man. Some years ago, when his eyesight was better, he had driven an old Studebaker pickup from the farm to Southern California. The engine had long since given up but the body was in pretty good shape, so he'd taken it to a welding shop, where they had lopped off the back end and added a hitch, converting it to a trailer where a large chest freezer now quietly hummed.

"This afternoon, we need to hook this trailer up to the car, go to the grocery store and buy enough ice cream to fill the freezer," Granddad said. This adventure was getting more interesting by the minute.

After a meager lunch, we hooked up the trailer and departed for the local Alpha Beta grocery store. When I moved to get behind the wheel, Granddad pushed me aside, insisting on driving, stating that he knew where the store was. His rationale eluded me. If he knew where the store was, couldn't he give me directions? Or, could he find the store only if he was behind the wheel taking traffic signal directions from me? The trip to the store was as choppy as our conversation which was punctuated with "green," "yellow," "red," "stop here!" and "you can go now." Granddad parked near the front door so we could make a quick getaway with our perishable cargo. The old Dodge with the Studebaker truck trailer in tow conjured a modern day image of *The Grapes of Wrath.*

Granddad wasn't particular about his ice cream. We stripped Alpha Beta's freezer bare, checking out with three shopping carts of ice cream. Butter brickle, vanilla, chocolate, chocolate chip, Neapolitan, strawberry, sherbet; you name it, we bought it. The checkout clerk gave us a quizzical look, the old farmer in his overalls and the sunburned college kid buying nothing but ice cream. Granddad really liked his ice cream!! We quickly transported the ice cream to the freezer under the hot California sun and hurried back to the house, but this time I drove as Granddad wanted me to get used to the feel of the car with the trailer in tow.

When we pulled into the driveway, Grandma was busily making peanut butter and jelly sandwiches for the trip.

"We'll have enough sandwiches to get us from here to Laramie," she said.

Granddad replied, "That's good, we won't need to stop at any restaurants or stores along the way. Not only will we save money, but we can keep moving. The way I have it figured, if we don't stop, other than for gas, the ice cream should stay frozen. When we drove here from Wyoming last spring, we stayed in a motel in Fillmore, Utah that didn't charge me to plug in the freezer for the night. Most places charge 25¢, so we have to make it to Fillmore tomorrow."

I didn't ask how far Fillmore was, but I was about to find out. The next morning, our feet were on the floor before sunrise.

"We want to get across the desert before it gets too hot," Granddad explained as we drove north of Riverside into the desert. Granddad had covered the trailer with a dark green army blanket to insulate it against the blistering desert heat. A dark blanket on a white freezer in the desert sun didn't seem to make much sense, but who was I to question? I was just the driver.

The old Dodge had a mind of its own. The weight of the trailer on the hitch, plus a trunk full of luggage and miscellaneous cargo strained the rear suspension. The front wheels, on the other hand, hardly seemed to touch the road. They just provided direction which was probably a good thing since the front tires were so worn that the cords were showing. Not wanting to waste money on accessories (or tires), Granddad's car consisted of little more than an engine and four wheels. The car did have one option, the most sensitive power steering in North America. The slightest movement of the steering wheel caused the front wheels to turn, which, in turn, caused the trailer to whip back and forth. I realized that it would take great finesse if I was going to stay out of the ditch for the next 1,000 miles as the car and trailer were at odds with each other every inch of the way. Granddad couldn't see the speedometer but he frequently asked me how fast I was driving. If I allowed the speed to drop below 65 mph he would remind me about our precious cargo and the freezer's date that night with a free electrical outlet in Utah.

Granddad hadn't accounted for road construction in his time calculations. Interstate 15, the main route from Southern California to Salt Lake City, was only partially completed in 1970. What wasn't complete was either under construction or a two-lane road. The trip from Riverside to Las Vegas took longer than expected, and Granddad was very anxious.

As we drove down the famous Las Vegas strip, he commented, "I'm glad we have food with us so we don't have to stop here and waste our time and money. This place is the devil's playground."

I, on the other hand, thought the air-conditioned casinos and restaurants looked pretty enticing from the old Dodge where the only air came through the open windows from the hot asphalt. Before long, the glitz of the strip was behind us and we headed into the desert. Granddad must have realized I'd have a hard time eating and steering the car at the same time because he asked, "If you'd like to stop for lunch, there's a rest stop ahead."

We pulled into a rest stop with one spindly desiccated tree and no restroom facilities. As I pulled the car to a stop, Granddad ordered Grandma to "Get out those sandwiches, we don't want to waste any time here." As we sat in the car, which was quickly starting to feel like an oven on wheels, Granddad reiterated, "I'm sure glad we have these sandwiches with us so we don't have to stop in a restaurant and waste our time and money."

I couldn't have disagreed more, but who was I to say anything? I was just the driver. When I signed up for this adventure, I hadn't planned on slowly baking in the Nevada desert while eating a peanut butter and jelly sandwich.

We downed lunch and hit the road, next stop St. George, Utah. The road from Las Vegas to St. George rises gradually, becoming steeper as it cuts through a corner of Arizona and nears Utah. The old Dodge started to overheat as the engine strained to pull the trailer uphill in the 100-degree heat. When Granddad asked how fast we were going I told him we were going slower than sixty-five because the car was overheating.

He said, "No it isn't, this car doesn't overheat!" Maybe not, but this was the first time the car had pulled a trailer with a freezer full of ice cream through the desert. Fortunately, there were some downhill stretches that gave the car a chance to cool off. Knowing Granddad couldn't see the speedometer, I kept the speed below sixty-five as we went up hills figuring what he didn't know wouldn't hurt him. When he asked how fast we were going I'd say "about sixty-five" and he seemed satisfied. Grandma sat in the back, where she could see the speedometer, not saying a word but no doubt chuckling to herself as I dealt with the unyielding stubbornness she'd lived with for almost fifty years.

We limped into St. George and stopped at a gas station, our first refill since leaving California. The old Dodge had a very large gas tank and it was all but empty. The attendant offered to check the oil but Granddad refused his offer. If the car didn't overheat it probably didn't use oil either. In a rare show of tenderness, Granddad then asked Grandma if she'd like something to drink. She had been sitting quietly in the car for the last 300 miles and was, no doubt, thirsty. She responded "that would be nice" and I assumed Granddad would get her a bottle of soda from the old chest cooler in the station. Instead, he rummaged through the trunk, retrieving an old empty cardboard milk carton, taking it to the men's room and filling it with water. He wasn't a man to dote on his wife.

We were on the final leg of the first day and I was beginning to tire. The temperature was significantly lower as we drove into Fillmore. We parked in front of the motel and Granddad went to the office to make arrangements for our night's lodging. The first order of business was to get the freezer settled in for the night which entailed backing the trailer into the parking space in front of our room. After several unsuccessful attempts, I finally got it right. Granddad plugged in the freezer and it started to hum. We checked the ice cream and, while soft, it was still frozen. Our room was small with knotty pine paneling, mottled brown and white linoleum floor tiles, a bathroom that had been "sanitized for our protection" and generously stocked with wafer-size bars of Ivory Soap, a black and white TV and a gold nubby bedspread on the sagging double bed. Noticeably lacking was a bed for me.

I tentatively asked Granddad, "Where am I supposed to sleep?"

"That's a good question," he responded, "I didn't ask when I got the room. We're only paying for two people and they might charge more for a third."

He peered into the closet and pulled his head out stating, "There's a blanket in there and an extra pillow too. You can sleep on the floor at the foot of the bed."

Not the best accommodation, but then again, I was just the driver. After a picnic of peanut butter and jelly sandwiches on a nubby gold tablecloth we turned in for the night as the sun set in the western sky. The double blanket was big enough that I could lie on one half and pull the other half over me. The linoleum floor was unyielding, and by morning, I felt like the room's third senior citizen.

Granddad must have been tiring of PB&J because he suggested that we have breakfast at a restaurant in Fillmore before heading north. As we loaded the car, I conjured images of a sumptuous breakfast of bacon, eggs and pancakes washed down with a glass of freshly squeezed orange juice. The small restaurant must not have been listed in the tourist literature for Fillmore. When we walked in the door, the busy natter of farmers and businessmen discussing the day's problems came to a stop and all eyes turned to us, the strangers in town. We were directed to a booth and the waitress placed three menus on the table and asked if we'd like coffee.

"That won't be necessary," Granddad retorted, no doubt worrying about the cost of such an extravagant meal.

The first item on the menu was bacon and scrambled eggs with toast. I wondered if the eggs were unadulterated or if they were fortified with soda crackers. Granddad asked me to read the menu to him as he couldn't see it. It was soon evident that my sumptuous breakfast plans were out the window for he scowled every time I read the price of an item. The cheapest entree on the menu was oatmeal so that's what we had. Eggs were expensive in Utah! After washing down our oatmeal with water, Granddad asked for the check. He got up and headed for the cashier without leaving a tip so I hung back and placed some change on the table. As we left the restaurant I caught the waitress's eye as she smiled and quietly uttered, "Thank you."

I could hear the din of morning conversation resume as the door closed behind us and we headed for the old Dodge.

Day number two was less eventful than day number one. Our final destination was my family's ranch near Laramie, about 500 miles distant, and the site of the freezer's next date with an electrical outlet. Temperatures were much cooler, which seemed to be more to the old Dodge's liking. While I had made peace with the power steering, an occasional twitch would send the trailer whipping back and forth until I was able to bring it back in alignment with the car and the road. We went through Salt Lake City about noon. By now I had given up any hopes of lunch in a restaurant, and my thoughts were set on a homemade dinner at the ranch that evening. Granddad was less vocal about Salt Lake than he was about Las Vegas, making a few comments about the Mormons and how they stored a year's worth of food in their cellars. During the height of the cold war, he had built a bomb shelter on the farm, and I was curious about what culinary delights it contained. Lots of dried eggs and crackers I supposed.

We had our last meal of PB&J at a rest area near the Utah-Wyoming border and settled into the car for the last leg of the trip. The road was good with the exception of a few sections that were under construction. We made good time and pulled into the ranch at about dinner time. The trees, the river, the mountains and my mom's cooking couldn't have looked better. We plugged in the freezer and washed up for dinner. Oddly enough, the fact that we had just driven 1,000 miles with a freezer full of ice cream never came up during our discussion of the trip. It wasn't until years later that I thought this a bit odd. When gas prices are cheap and there's money to be saved, I guess there's really no need to discuss what obviously made sense at the time.

As we finished a meal of freshly caught trout from the river, my mom asked, "Would anyone like some dessert? I have fruit and cookies but I think we're out of ice cream."

Knowing there was a freezer full of ice cream outside, I waited for Granddad to make a dessert offering. He didn't make a move and we satisfied ourselves with fruit and cookies. He'd paid 39¢ a half gallon for that cache of ice cream, and he wasn't about to share it with anyone else! The next morning, he and Grandma got in the car to drive the final 150 miles to the farm in Veteran. I worried about them as they drove out of the yard, but they knew the way. Despite the fact that the driver was virtually blind, there weren't many stoplights along the way, and they still had a supply of road weary sandwiches should they get hungry en route.

The Kiss
Sharon Fish

Joe Polchies emigrated from Indian Island, Old Town, Maine. I don't know the circumstances of his move to Bar Harbor, but I do know he was a tall, dark, ruggedly handsome, athletic American Indian who got Nancy Higgins pregnant, after which she dropped out of school, married him, and gave birth to Marie. Joe remained in high school, earning his diploma and all the accolades due a football and basketball star. After graduation, he worked as a sales clerk at Sachsman's Men's Clothing Store, owned and operated by Mort Sachsman, who would later shoot himself to death after hours to avoid the inevitable ramifications of an inoperable brain tumor, a medical condition his wife and children learned of after Mort's death. It was a quality store that catered to bricklayers, businessmen, and girls like me, who bought wheat-colored boys' Levi's and blue chambray work shirts. Joe and Nancy rented the attached apartment behind Sachsman's store.

I met the couple through my best friend Patty, who was a babysitter for their two babies, Marie and Johnny. There was something naively tantalizing in knowing someone who *had* to get married, who had had premarital sex, something remote and mysterious to me. Funny and friendly, Nancy was petite, pretty with dark, curly hair, blue eyes, and peachy skin. I liked being around her and began babysitting when Patty was not available. Eventually, Patty and I began alternating when Joe and Nancy wanted to go out for an evening, to a movie, a party, or a dance. They paid me fifty cents an hour, and they trusted me with their children. Although it would have been a mere ten-minute walk, Joe insisted on driving me home.

"Your father wouldn't want you walking home this late," he said.

I didn't object, even though it was only ten o'clock on a summer night. I felt as safe as Jem and Scout Finch did in Maycomb, Alabama. I knew every street and shortcut in town, and I was not afraid of tourists. In fact, the only person who gave me the creeps, and I was not alone, was Mr. C, a short, wiry man who stared at children with his beady eyes and muttered to himself. Dealing with him was simply a matter of crossing the street or avoiding eye contact rather than making an awkward dash. He had a small timid wife and a beautiful dark eyed young daughter. What their lives were like was a curiosity and a mystery. But, for the most part, it was a congenial town with the usual social stratifications. When the sidewalks were rolled up, after tourist season, everybody knew everybody, more or less.

We walked to Joe's blue Ford. He held the door for me. I don't remember what we talked about, or rather what he talked about. As comfortable as I was in my town, in the woods, and along the ocean, I was uncomfortable with adults, especially men, even Joe Polchies who was only five years older than I. Both a smoker and a slacker, he was probably lecturing me on the pitfalls of cigarettes or the benefits of earning good grades. We drove down Cottage Street, stopped briefly at the flashing red traffic light, the only one in town, turned right onto Main Street and right again onto Newton Way, and then left onto Des Isle Avenue, a short street that boasts nine houses and the back side of McKay's Motel, a single storied affair for the economically minded – a street so narrow it made a Volkswagen Beetle look imposing. The street where my sister and I paraded on stilts, for hours at a time. The street on which Juanita Warren taught me to ride my new English bicycle, a sleek, black model that was to be my only mode of transportation all the way through high school. The street on which, out of direst boredom on a scorching summer day, Sandra and I squatted or lay to pop tar bubbles. The street on which we played hopscotch, kickball, and jacks. We never worried much about traffic; our neighbors knew to watch out for us.

He pulled up and parked in front of number nine, a rented two- story duplex where I lived with my mother, father, sister, and brother. I stepped from the car and closed its door, but not before Joe had emerged from the driver's side and appeared at the front of the car, saying, "I was going to open the door for you, Sharon." He had a deep voice with an ironic lisp. His approach was fast. Pushing his hands on my shoulders and pressing the weight of his large body tight against my fourteen-year old smallness, he leaned his face down to mine, forced his open mouth over mine, forced my mouth open, and forced his tongue into my mouth, grinding his teeth against mine. He reeked of alcohol and power. I was paralyzed. I dreaded what might happen next. Nothing did. When it ended, he pressed a sweaty, folded bill in my hand. He had been holding it all along. "Don't tell anyone about this, Sharon," he said. I could see the glow of the living room lights through the curtained windows. I somehow wished Maurice Carter, our nosy duplex neighbor, had been spying just then, but apparently he had not.

"I won't," I answered. And I did not. Joe drove away as I climbed the three steps of our wooden front porch, the porch where I read Nancy Drew stories, and *Gone with the Wind*, and *A Christmas Carol*. My father, in his brown, faux leather recliner was facing the television and the curtain-covered windows that looked out onto Des Isle Avenue. "Hi, Dad, Hi Mum," I said entering the front hall. My mother was in her usual spot at the far end of the sofa, painting her elegant, memorable nails in the soft light of the table lamp. I did not take my place next to her. Instead, I climbed the stairs to the yellow flowered bedroom I shared with my sister. I could not tell Sandra, for she would tell my mother, who would tell my father, who would, in defense of me, lose his temper and would lose in any kind of altercation he might have with Joe Polchies. He would have wanted to beat him up. I could not bear the idea. Nor did I tell Nancy, Joe's wife. I wanted to protect her, too. There was also the shame. I opened the bill in my hand. Five dollars. I wanted to take a bath, but I did not. It wasn't Sunday night.

Ode to Humanity
Barbie LaMarca

It's hard to be good
For goodness' sake.
Those making the effort
Might appear somewhat fake.

It's easy to ridicule
To judge and to spurn;
But...the harvest from this
Is a bitter return.

What does it matter
The color of skin?
Earth is the bowl
We all find ourselves in.

People are born
And someday dead.
All need a roof
And a loaf of bread.

All feel pain
And heat and cold.
All feel anxious
As their lives unfold

The inner spirit
Knows no gender.
One is hard,
Another tender.

Life flings its evils
At every turn.
How to avoid them
Is tough to learn.

It matters to me.
It should matter to you—
What people worldwide
Are apt to do.

While nature whirls
And writhes and spumes—
Don't add to the chaos
With toxic fumes.

Don't just sit
In disgust or disgrace!
Do your part—
Build a better place.

Expressing a kindness,
In thought, then deed—
Is quenching the thirst
Of universal need.

In the waning hours,
As you reflect—
You'll want to regard
Your life with respect.

Though it's hard to be good
For goodness' sake—
To do otherwise
Is a costly mistake.

Henry's World
Barbie LaMarca

Chapter 1

Golden rays streamed through the branches of the huge willow tree and onto the kitchen table. It was the beginning of a new day for Henry as he rubbed the sand from the corners of his eyes.

"Henry, eat your breakfast," his mother said.

"But Mommy, I'm not hungry right now. Can I go outside first?"

"Great explorers need energy for their journeys." she said.

Henry quickly crunched his toast as the jelly smudged the edges of his lips. He gulped down the glass of milk, adding a white mustache over the jelly.

He bolted from the chair and crouched down to put on his sneakers — still covered with the mud from yesterdays' explorations.

"Don't forget to wash your face and brush your teeth," his mother said.

"Aw, Mommy, do I have to?"

"Henry!" she warned.

He quickly brushed his teeth and left the cap and the unrinsed toothbrush in the sink.

Bounding out the door, he took the path to the pond, where there were always so many creatures and happenings. He would check the green chrysalises to see if they were open yet. He was anxious to see what type of butterfly would take form.

He loved watching the little green frogs that had suckers on the pads of their feet. They could climb everything – even upside down – and never fall off.

When turtles' heads bobbed above the water, then disappeared, he imagined they were playing hide-and-seek with him.

He turned over a dead tree root and was amazed as hundreds of scurrying bugs were uncovered — there were so many different shapes and sizes. The snails and grubs didn't move much at all.

This is so cool! Henry thought. At the pond there were so many things to be curious about.

"I can't wait to show Sam some of the things I've found!"

Chapter 2

Henry ran back to the house for his knapsack. His cheeks were pink and he was nearly breathless. His knapsack was dark green with smudges of brown dirt and yellow pollen from his many adventures.

In his sack were his special boxes and jars. Some were for critters, some were for plants. He would capture crawly or swimmy things in the jars. Turtles or eggs or branches with chrysalises he would put in boxes with holes on the top to make sure his specimens could breathe.

"I'm going to Sam's house!" Henry yelled to his mother. Mommy had gone to school with Sam when she was Henry's age.

Henry hurried back to the pond and turned the log over again. He wanted to catch one of the long orange bugs with lots of legs on each side of its body. He remembered his mother telling him not to touch creatures he didn't know about because they might hurt him. So, he used his lids to direct the bugs into his jars. He made sure to coax a brown spider with a fiddle on its back into another jar.

He worked very hard to catch one of the little green frogs and gently placed it in one of his boxes.

Finally, he snapped off one of the branches that held a chrysalis and put it into another box.

He walked very carefully to Sam's house. Sam was a science teacher at the high school. He did not have a child of his own and was happy to spend time with Henry.

Behind the big white farmhouse was an even bigger red barn with very squeaky doors. This is where Sam had a huge room with microscopes and hundreds of jars with something interesting in each one.

He also had a few cages with squirrels, rabbits or birds in them. People would bring Sam animals that were sick or hurt. He would try to help them and keep them safe until they were ready to go free in the woods again. Henry was always excited to see what Sam had in his cages.

"Hey, Henry! What did you bring for us to study, today?"

Chapter 3

Henry took his jars and boxes out of his knapsack. He showed Sam his creepy crawlies and the chrysalis.

Sam said, "Let's take a look at this orange bug with all the legs."

He went to his many shelves of books and pulled out one about insects. He handed it to Henry.

"Flip through the pages and see if you can find a picture of a bug like yours."

After a few minutes, Henry shouted, "I found it! This looks just like my bug. It's called a 'centipede'."

"Would you like to know why it's called that?" asked Sam. "There is a very old language called Latin. Many of our words have parts of Latin words in them. There are two parts to the name of your bug – 'centi' which means 100 and 'pede' which means foot. Let's see what else the book tells us about it. It has thin skin so it needs to stay in a moist, dark place. Where did you find it?"

"I found it under a dead tree root. There were lots of these and many other bugs."

"You have to be careful when you handle these. They have tiny claws in the first section of their bodies that contain poison. You could get quite a bad bite from one."

Next, Henry opened one of his boxes and tried to lift out the green frog, but it jumped from his hands onto Sam's face!

"Whoa!" Sam's eyes opened very wide in surprise. The little frog's foot pads were sucking his face and it felt funny. He gently handed it back to Henry.

"Let's put away the insect book and find one about amphibians. This word also comes from Latin meaning 'both sides'. A frog is an amphibian because it can live in both environments—underwater and on the ground. It can breathe in both places."

"I think I found it – it's called a Green Tree Frog. This diagram shows its special feet. Its body is usually 1-2 inches long. It eats insects, has smooth skin and makes a loud quacking sound. Hey, this is cool! Its body can change to different shades of green depending on the temperature and light."

Suddenly, they heard the clanging of the farmhouse bell. They opened the barn door and looked over at the porch. Sam's wife, Olivia, was holding the rope.

"Lunch is ready for you two explorers. You can wash your hands at the well. If I know you, you've been touching all kinds of dirty things."

On the round table in the middle of the bright kitchen were bologna and cheese sandwiches, a bowl of fruit and a plate with three different kinds of cookies.

"Would you like lemonade or milk with your lunch, boys?"

"Lemonade, please," said Henry.

When they finished lunch, Henry helped Sam take the dishes to the sink and wash them.

"Thank you, Olivia! That was delicious — especially the double chocolate chip cookies!"

Back in the barn Sam took Henry over to a cage with a medium sized wild rabbit that was missing a big chunk of her ear.

"This, here, is Meadow. She apparently got into a fight with a fox. I can tell by the shape of the teeth marks on the bitten ear. It took three weeks for it to heal. I think she's ready to go home. Would you like to come with me to set her free?"

"Yeah!" exclaimed Henry.

They walked quite a way into the woods. When she was released, Meadow hopped quickly in the direction of her warren. Henry knew she was happy to be out of that cage.

It had been quite a day. Henry was very tired. He went home, washed up, had dinner and put on his truck pajamas. His head touched the pillow and he fell asleep right away.

My Wilderness Experience
Ted King
A lesson in brain injury survival; loss and grief; healing prayers and dreams; forgiveness, faith, hope, and love; recovery and rebirth as a minister and witness of Jesus' healing grace.

On Sunday March 23rd, 2003, I suffered a massive stroke. Without having any known risk factors for a stroke, and being in good physical condition, this took my family and me by complete surprise. It also took my independence, my medical practice, and my ability to enjoy the sports I loved – particularly running, tennis, downhill skiing, and competitive sailboat racing.

My life since then has been a true wilderness experience. My family and I have been tested spiritually, emotionally, physically, and financially in significantly discouraging ways.

My faith in my prospects for surviving the stroke (I don't like to call it "my stroke") was strengthened by the timely presence of several "guardian angels," as I now call them, who were with me during critical, life-saving encounters in times of crisis.

The first such encounter was this: at the time of the stroke my older sister Kathy, and her husband, Jim, a psychiatrist, were visiting us from Boulder, Colorado. Jim was able to recognize the symptoms of a stroke in progress, even though it was very early morning and I was still in bed and barely awake. His quick thinking got me to the Exeter Hospital Emergency Room, where my second guardian angel, neurologist Kent Logan, MD, rapidly diagnosed an ischemic, right cerebral hemisphere stroke coming from a right internal artery blood clot. He administered the TPA clot buster drug within the critical three hours of stroke onset. Within five minutes of receiving that injection, I began moving my left arm and left leg. Thirdly, a vigilant ICU nurse noted anisocoria (unequal pupil diameter of my eyes) indicative of cerebral edema. I was immediately taken to the Lahey Clinic in Burlington, Massachusetts, where my brain swelling was closely monitored for many days. With vigilant observation and medication, while under the wise care of another neurologist, Claudia Chaves, MD, I successfully avoided a craniotomy (having my head cut open to relieve the pressure inside the skull).

As a result of this wilderness experience, I have delved into God's word in a new way. As I read the Bible now, I sense God speaking to me when Scripture verses resonate strongly within me. **1 Corinthians 10:13** tells me that "God is faithful and He will not allow you to be tested beyond your ability to endure. At the time you are put to the test, He will give you the strength to endure it, and so provide you with a way out."

I was supremely tested just about six months to the day after the stroke. My entire hemiplegic left side slowly became tight and in spasm. The worst of it was unremitting intense pain in one of my left toes. It was as if a knife were thrust under the toenail. The pain was unrelieved by postural change, drugs, sex, or alcohol! Perhaps most frustrating to me, as a traditional Western medical practitioner, was not having at hand a reliable modality for pain relief. I progressed quickly to desperate thinking, as in, "if this pain is my cross to bear, it's not a life I want to lead." Suicidal ideation soon followed. While my mind was preoccupied with how to end this suffering, I did not lose faith in my likelihood of finding the answer. I just prayed harder for God's help.

That help came in the form of yet another guardian angel, my mailman George King, whom I'd encounter between 2:00 and 3:00 pm on my daily walk around the neighborhood, and with whom I had shared my muscle spasm malady. One day he stopped his old blue beater of a Subaru and said, "Doc, I want to give you something. Here," passing me a blue ballpoint pen with a name printed on it. "This lady, a Chinese acupuncturist near Boston, worked wonders relieving my back pain spasms from the Vietnam War. You'll like her," he promised. "We Kings have to stick together," he added, as he drove away.

"Bingo!" I thought. "That's the answer I've been seeking." I knew from my 25 years of clinical practice in orthopedics and hand surgery, that acupuncture had indeed been effective for some of my patients. With confidence that my answer was at hand, I searched for an acupuncturist closer to home. I was referred to Jeanne Ann Whittington in Concord, NH. I'll admit I was a bit skeptical that this Caucasian eastern medical practitioner with a soft Texas drawl was the one for me. However, after the first painless encounter with needles, there was, indeed, less pain. After my second visit I was pain free. Hallelujah!

Shortly after my wife's mother died of a stroke in August, 2006, I attended a bereavement seminar series with my wife at a local church. There, and in reading the Bible, I learned that unforgiveness can be a major block to healing. I realized that I was angry with my body for failing me. I've had to forgive myself. This, I believe, was a major turning point in my recovery journey.

Proverbs 3: 5-6 has been a guide for me. "Trust in the Lord with all your heart and lean not on your own understanding; in all your ways acknowledge him and he will make your paths straight." I'm relying on God like never before.

Jeremiah tells me in Chapter 29 Verse 11: "For I know the plans I have for you, declares the Lord. Plans to prosper you and not to harm you. Plans to give you hope and a future."

We know from the book of Exodus that Moses spoke face to face with God on Mt. Sinai while he and the people of Israel wandered for 40 years through the wilderness. I, too, speak with God (if not exactly face to face) as I walk through the neighborhood. One day I prayed, "Lord, my skills for your purpose." I beseeched Him to guide me to a place where I can now serve. The result is what I call my sidewalk consultative medical practice, or, "healing by proxy!"

My greatest success in this new ministry came when my neighbor, Neil, needed surgical intervention to relieve his desperately painful condition of intractable ulnar nerve pain. Neil had fallen from the storage space above his garage, landing on the concrete floor below and shattering his elbow. Later on, after the bone had healed, his ulnar nerve became entrapped by scar tissue. Neil's pain was an 11 on a scale of 1-10. He was unable to work or sleep. He was close to the end of his rope. His hand therapists at Access Sports Medicine and Orthopedics in Exeter suggested he talk with me. I referred him to Jesse Jupiter, MD, an orthopedic trauma specialist at Massachusetts General Hospital, who would treat this complicated problem, if not personally, then by referring Neil to a specialist who could. It turned out that Dr. Jupiter referred Neil to his colleague, Johnathan Winograd, MD, a peripheral nerve specialist, who, in a lengthy procedure, freed the ulnar nerve from the scar tissue and protected it from further entrapment with a venous allograft wrap. Neil's pain diminished. He's back to normal – at work and in his garden. Hallelujah!

Using this "healing by proxy," I've been able to answer medical questions and suggest referrals for others to find medical care using my pre-stroke network of colleagues. Thank you, Lord, for using my skills to help others.

In Job 33:15 we read that God speaks to us in visions and dreams. I believe that God was speaking to me one night in a dream soon after the stroke.

In my dream I find myself at sea level in a predawn dark harbor. The waters around me are flat, calm, and temperate. Filling the harbor are numerous sturdy, yet majestic, three-masted sailing ships lying at anchor, their sails neatly furled at the yardarm. The only sounds are of waves lapping gently against the hulls, a light breeze whistling quietly though their rigging lines, and the creaking of their hawsers at the bow chocks. I have the distinct, but subconscious, impression that these ships are about to weigh anchor, setting forth on their own perilous oceanic journeys. I now know that this harbor was God's own harbor, or sanctuary, where all is safe and quiet.

I, too, was about to embark on a long, personal journey following this stroke, which had so injured my brain. In my dream that fateful night, I sensed that God would remain with me, watching over and protecting me during this voyage. I recall saying prayers to God, with words to the effect of, "Dear Lord, if you bring me through this stroke, and whatever it entails, I will be a witness to your healing grace."

I hope that in some way today I'm fulfilling that promise I made to God several years ago.

Beyond the Ceiling
Marilyn Page

Helen Keller said, "One can never consent to creep, when one has an impulse to soar."

Have you ever wanted to soar, at something? How can you make that happen? And what would it feel like?

Last year, on a bright summer day, I was cleaning out my garage. I'd opened the two garage doors, two side windows and a side door. I wanted the clean breeze to blow out the musty winter smells. As I was bent down working on a project, I suddenly heard a loud buzz over my head. Certain that I was about to be attacked by a swarm of bees, I decided I had better see exactly where they were, so I'd know in which direction to run for cover. As I looked, to my relief and delight I found myself nose-to-beak with a ruby throated hummingbird, whom I immediately named Ruby. Ruby buzzed around the garage, inspected a bright red plant pot sitting on a high shelf that was still full of soil, then decided he'd seen enough. The day was much too nice to be inside my messy garage; he needed to get outside and soar. And up he went. Unfortunately, Ruby's attempt to soar was stopped short as he bumped his head on the garage ceiling.

Twenty years ago my public speaking skills were non-existent. I was petrified of the mere thought of speaking before a group. I'd tried putting myself in situations where I'd have to speak, but I never made much progress. Like Ruby, I kept hitting my head on the ceiling, and I was going nowhere fast.

Back in my garage, Ruby's head was getting sore. He'd now spent about six hours banging into the ceiling. Though I kept telling him about the open doors and windows, he lacked listening skills. I even left him alone, thinking that would encourage him to fly low and leave. That didn't work either. Exhausted, he finally rested his beautiful little body on the edge of the plant pot. He was so tired he just looked down at me as if to say, "I'm done. I can't do it. I need help." I slowly and quietly approached him. His little chest was heaving as I gently picked up the pot and walked to the nearest open window. I held the pot out the window with one hand, and with the other gave him a slight nudge to fly away.

November 1995 I hit my ceiling with full force! I was at the hospital reading Psalm 116 with my dear uncle who was dying. When we finished reading, he and my aunt thought it would be meaningful if I would read the Psalm at his funeral service. Of course, I said yes. Wouldn't you have done the same? I left the room, walked outside to the parking lot and got into my car. There, I sat down on the edge of my plant pot, and my insides began to heave from panic. I knew I lacked the skills necessary to speak confidently before a group, especially at such an emotional time as a funeral service. Just like Ruby needed me to carry him to the window and nudge him in the right direction, I needed help to overcome my fear of public speaking. I joined Toastmasters International, a public speaking organization, and I began to learn some much needed speaking skills.

As I watched Ruby fly away that day, I expected him to vanish quickly, but he didn't. He flew at one level for a while, as if to take everything in, then he'd step up a notch. And so it would go – one level, then up, as though in slow motion. His soaring was gradual and intentional. And I believe that day his soaring was all the sweeter, for he knew what he'd been missing while trapped in my garage.

Eventually the time arrived for me to read the Psalm at my uncle's funeral. Sad but confident, I walked up to the lectern and faced family and friends. I shared a little story about him and then read the Psalm. That day my improved speaking skills had allowed me to keep my promise to my aunt and uncle, and I was starting to soar. Over the years I've continued to develop those skills, which have broadened my life both personally and professionally

Unknowingly, that day in the hospital my aunt and uncle had taken me to the window's edge and invited me to soar. My communication skills have been the wings that have kept moving me up, one level at a time.

What ceilings are you bumping into? Determine the skills you might need to develop that will take you in a new direction or help you reach a goal. Then gradually, and intentionally, enjoy the exhilaration of soaring.

Loneliness and Snow
The Magic of Robert Frost
Don Nolte

New Englanders embrace poet laureate Robert Frost, reciting his works at library gatherings and writers' groups. They read him to their grandchildren, the magic of his words helping generations bridge their gap. Frost's appeal seems to lie in the clarity of his depiction of rural scenes, often with a specter of loneliness, inability to find brotherhood, but somehow arriving at a feeling of reconciliation, of humanity finding its way despite the fears.

"Something there is that doesn't love a wall," Frost writes, yet he notes that walls are repaired again and again, by neighbors who seem to want them.

"The Fear" evokes a nameless dread, inspired by loneliness. "Snow" presents a mood of loneliness and separation, but with hope of overcoming it. Snow is depicted as a "pallid thing" that has "died against the window pane." It is the catalyst, "glancing off the roof, Making a great scroll upward toward the sky, Long enough for recording all our names on." Playing on the poet's name, "You see the snow-white through the white of frost?" The evangelistic Meserve must venture into the blizzard: "There is a sort of tunnel in the frost ... way down at the far end of it you see a stir and quiver like the frayed edge of the drift blown in the wind. I like that."

Fear of loneliness permeates Frost's words like frost, chilling, numbing, driving to remorse. We feel compassion for lonely Silas in "Death of the Hired Man" and John's frustrated hopes in "The Housekeeper." "Home Burial" depicts a failure to communicate, and in "The Hill Wife" we see sadness:

> One ought not to have to care
> So much as you and I,
> Care when the birds come round the house
> To seem to say good-bye;
> Or care so much when they come back
> With whatever it is they sing;
>
> The truth being we are as much
> Too glad for the one thing
> As we are too sad for the other here -
> With birds that fill their breasts
> But with each other and themselves
> And their built or driven nests.

In "Desert Places" Frost hauntingly juxtaposes intrapersonal loneliness with intrapersonal emptiness:

> And lonely as it is, that loneliness
> Will be more lonely ere it will be less -
> A blanker whiteness of benighted snow
> With no expression, nothing to express.

> They cannot scare me with their empty spaces
> Between stars - on stars where no human race is.
> I have it in me so much nearer home
> To scare myself with my own desert places.

Often, Frost's characters seek to ignore or deny their fears. In "An Old Man's Winter Night": "What kept him from remembering the need, That brought him to that creaking room was age. He stood with barrels round him - at a loss." "The Figure in the Doorway" denies loneliness, as does "the Gum-Gatherer." Even in "Desert Places," the reciter challenges the its effect: "I am too absent-spirited to count; The loneliness includes me unawares." In "Revelation" Frost observes that men seek to retreat behind a facade of light words, "But oh, the agitated heart, Til someone really find us out" and what a "pity if the case require (Or so we say) that in the end We speak the literal to inspire The understanding of a friend."

Despite grappling with fears, Frost does express idealist views, as in "Two Tramps in Mud Time": "My object in living is to unite My avocation and my vocation As my two eyes make one in sight; Only where love and need are one, And the work is play for mortal stakes, Is the deed ever really done, For Heaven and the future's sakes." And often there is a suggestion of redemption in the end, as expressed in "Dust of Snow": "The way a crow Shook down on me The dust of snow From a hemlock tree Has given my heart a change of mood and saved some part of a day I had rued."

And Frost finds hope that men are not so separate after all. In "Tuft of Flowers" loneliness is dispelled by a butterfly and a tuft of weed, "a message from the dawn, ... that made me hear the wakening birds around,"

> And hear his long scythe whispering to the ground,
> And feel a spirit kindred to my own;
> So that henceforth I worked no more alone;
> But glad with him, I worked as with his aid,

And weary, sought at noon with him the shade;
And dreaming, as it were, held brotherly speech
With one whose thought I had not hoped to reach.
'Men work together,' I told him from the heart,
'Whether they work together or apart.'

In "A Considerable Speck" Frost relates, "No one can know how glad I am to find On any sheet the least display of mind." And "In the Clearing" observes, "It takes all kinds of in and outdoor schooling To get adapted to my kind of fooling." Frost describes having a "lover's quarrel with the world." Though he revels in simplicity, he is never naive. Robert Frost "took the road less traveled by," and therein lies his charm.

Rattlesnake Roundup
Ursula Nolte

The rattlesnake roundup is a famous tradition in Texas. Ranchers go into the countryside to gather rattlesnakes, then display them before an audience. By handling these reptiles they seek to demonstrate courage and bravery. After they have achieved this goal, the snakes are destroyed.

This celebrated event has become a controversial issue. One group claims it is only a harmless sport; the other declares it cruel and inhumane.

Many years ago I would have sided with the first group. I had heard stories of people being attacked and bitten by rattlesnakes. Usually the person died or was disfigured. I was very much afraid of snakes for this reason. I came to the conclusion that rattlesnakes and all other poisonous snakes were a threat to mankind, and we had a right to kill them randomly.

In the story of Adam and Eve in the Bible the snake is pictured in a negative way. It is the voice of temptation, and through its interference in paradise Adam and Eve become separated from their harmony with God. The image of the snake seems to be connected with sin, death and distress in our world. Therefore, I thought the snake is an evil creature that must be destroyed.

Even though I am not a snake lover, I view those subjects differently today. I believe poisonous snakes have a right to live and should not be killed randomly.

In nature books I have read about snakes and their habits. Most of the poisonous snakes are not as aggressive as they were once described. If people would be more careful and observant when they enter a snake habitat, fewer accidents would happen.

I also learned that snakes play an important role in controlling the rodent population. If too many snakes are killed, an imbalance in nature occurs that can cause problems for farmers and our environment.

Through my study of the demythologization of the Bible I also changed my childish belief that the snake "per se" must be evil. The snake in the Bible is meant only as a symbol. The reptile as we see it in nature is neither good nor bad. It is in fact God's creation, created for our good.

Biologists have observed that the rattlesnake population in Texas has diminished in recent years. If the rattlesnake roundups continue, we have to face the reality that one day the Texas rattlesnake may be among many extinct species – and this through the ignorance and negligence of people who do not care for the environment and the future of our world. We do not want to let this happen.

On Being Late
John Kane

Earl Dowd had spent ten months in the womb,
Before he arrived in the delivery room.
It appeared that he was gifted with a trait
To sometimes be a little bit late.

At school he was marked for his tardy trends,
And was nicknamed "Early" by his friends.
His working life might have been sublime,
Had only he arrived to work on time.

In his later years he was self-employed.
He could choose his hours as he enjoyed.
As time went on, no friends were alive,
But Earl lived on until ninety-five.

He was even late for his funeral mass;
It seems the hearse ran out of gas.
In church there were snickers heard in the crowd,
When the pastor spoke of the "late Earl Dowd".

His arrival in heaven led to despair.
The gate was closed – no one was there.

It seemed to be an eternity for the time he had to wait.
Eventually Peter came with the key and opened the Pearly Gate.
"Here in heaven", he said with a wink and a grin, "It ain't no sin
to be a little late."

Not You

If your mother conceived
A month after she did,
It wouldn't be you,
But some other kid.

Richard E. Haskell

Spoken Words

The spoken word,
For good or ill,
Can change a life,
And dreams fulfill.

Richard E. Haskell

Alone

Quiet times,
All alone,
Often put me
In the zone.

Richard E. Haskell

Written Words

The written word
Fills many pages,
But can inspire,
Throughout the ages.

Richard E. Haskell

SPRING

THE QUIET SPRING,
LIKE A COILED SPRING,
SPRUNG THROUGH THE ICE,
ON THE FIRST DAY OF SPRING.

RICHARD E. HASKELL

Writers of the Round Table
Richard E. Haskell

There once was a group most eclectic,
A prompt, they will try to dissect it.
For as long as they're able,
They write at Norm's table.
A book in the end will collect it.

32572867R00070

Made in the USA
Middletown, DE
09 June 2016